# CONTENT EVERYWHERE
STRATEGY AND STRUCTURE FOR FUTURE-READY CONTENT

Sara Wachter-Boettcher

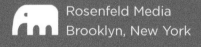

Rosenfeld Media
Brooklyn, New York

*Content Everywhere: Strategy and Structure for Future-Ready Content*

By Sara Wachter-Boettcher

Rosenfeld Media, LLC

457 Third Street, #4R

Brooklyn, New York

11215 USA

On the Web: www.rosenfeldmedia.com

Please send errors to: errata@rosenfeldmedia.com

Publisher: Louis Rosenfeld

Managing Editor: Marta Justak

Interior Layout Tech: Danielle Foster

Cover Design: The Heads of State

Indexer: Nancy Guenther

Proofreader: Sue Boshers

ISBN: 1-933820-87-X

ISBN-13: 978-1-933820-87-3

LCCN: 2012950613

Printed and bound in the United States of America

# DEDICATION

For William

# HOW TO USE THIS BOOK

## Who Should Read This Book?

This book is for anyone who cares about content and is interested in making it work for mobile devices, across multiple channels, and for an increasingly unfixed future.

You might consider yourself a content strategist, as I do. If so, as you strive for content that's useful, meaningful, and sustainable, this book will help you think about all the places that content might go: desktop computers, yes, but also mobile devices, read-later applications, social media platforms, and myriad other places we haven't even thought about yet.

Or, you might be an information architect or user experience designer tasked with structuring websites and designing navigation systems. In addition to designing macro systems for information, this book will show you how to construct more micro systems: structures within a single piece of content that allow you to do much more with it, from creating deep connections within a single site to building multiple products off the same core base of content.

If you're a writer or editor, this book is designed to get you thinking less about pages of content and where they'll "live" on a website, and more about the components that lend your content life. When you do, you'll discover that the best way to keep the story, message, or meaning of your content intact isn't to try to control how it looks on the page; it's to give it the underlying structure that will let it be styled and used in appropriate ways wherever it goes.

You might also be a content manager wrangling a big CMS. An SEO specialist. A mobile designer or developer who's trying to make your creations work with real content. Whatever your background or job title, if you want content that can go more places, more easily, then this book was written just for you. I hope you enjoy it.

## What's in This Book?

A couple hundred pages of ideas, models, concepts, tips, and a bunch of stories about people trying new ways to make their content work harder.

Practically speaking, though, this book is divided into four parts:

**Part I** explores the problems with content that is fixed and inflexible, and talks about how we can start looking at the content we create differently. It also defines how four key disciplines set a foundation for today's challenge: content strategy, information architecture, technical communications, and content management.

**Part II** is all about building a framework: a way of breaking content down, building it up in meaningful models, and understanding what's at play as it starts being used and reconfigured using everything from markup to media queries to APIs.

**Part III** digs into a few of the myriad things you can do with your content once you've sorted out how it's structured and stored: make content more findable and interconnected, make it work harder on responsive and adaptive sites, reuse it across multiple products and personalized experiences, and prepare it to even leave your control completely.

**Part IV** will leave you with a call to get started—not just with structuring your content, but with changing your organization and its relationship to content, too. With these skills, you can create content that's audience-centric, lively, and lovable—even as it is replicated and reused.

## What Comes with This Book?

This book's companion website (𝕸 rosenfeldmedia.com/books/content-everywhere/) contains some templates, discussion, and additional content. The book's diagrams and other illustrations are available under a Creative Commons license (when possible) for you to download and include in your own presentations. You can find these on Flickr at 𝕸 www.flickr.com/photos/rosenfeldmedia/sets/.

# FREQUENTLY ASKED QUESTIONS

### What do you mean by "content everywhere"?

The way I talk about it, "content everywhere" doesn't mean splattering your message in every corner of the Web. It's about investing in content that's flexible enough to go wherever you need it: multiple websites, apps, channels, and other experiences. Why? Because devices of all shapes, sizes, and capabilities are flooding the market, and users expect to get your content on all of them, which you can read about in Chapter 1.

Right now, most organizations can barely keep up with their large, unwieldy desktop websites, much less multiple different sets of content for all these different experiences. Content everywhere is all about learning how to prepare one set of content to go wherever it's needed—now and in the future.

### What do you mean by structured content, and why is it so important?

Today, most digital content is unstructured: just words poured onto a page. To signify where one part ends and another begins, writers use formatting, like upping a font size to be a headline or putting an author's name in italics. This works fine if your content is only going to be used on a single page and viewed on a desktop monitor, but that's about it.

Structured content, on the other hand, is created in smaller modules, which can be stored and used in lots more ways. For example, you could display a headline and a copy teaser in one place, and have a user click to read the rest—something you can't do if the story is all one blob. You can give the same content different presentation rules when it's displayed on mobile, such as resizing headlines or changing which content is prioritized or emphasized—automatically. In this way, adding structure actually makes content *more* flexible, because it allows you to do more with it. You can learn about this in Chapter 5.

### But don't I need different, simpler content for mobile?

If your content is needlessly complicated and full of fluff, then yes: Your content should be simplified for mobile—and for everywhere else, too. After all, a user with a desktop computer doesn't want to wade through filler either. But should your mobile users be offered "lite" versions of your content rather than the real deal? No.

While you might know what people do *most often* on their mobile devices, you can't know what they're intending to do on any *specific visit*. After all, people apply to college and buy cars on their phones every day—and will only do more on mobile as devices get more powerful and cheaper. Finally, I've seen firsthand how hard it can be for organizations to manage content on just one website. How much harder will it be when you're juggling updates and versions for multiple discrete experiences? There's no way you'll have the time, resources, and skills to keep up. One set of content that's clear, meaningful, and well structured is a more sustainable solution. You can read more about making this work in Chapters 9 and 10.

## Who should be doing this work?

In the past, content modeling work was often just called data modeling, so it was done by database developers. That's not necessarily a bad thing, but it has its problems. Because content can be much more ambiguous and conceptual than other sorts of data, it needs attention a developer alone is unlikely to give it. If you want content to communicate a message, tell a story, or do something specific for your organization or your users, then you need someone who understands what the content means and how it means it there when you're making content modeling decisions.

Oftentimes, the ideal person to play this role is a content strategist, editor, information architect, or user experience designer. The good news is, it's not either-or. Content modeling and structuring can and should be collaborative—something that's more effective when people from multiple perspectives are involved. In Chapters 3 and 4 of this book, I aim to show those who may not have been in those conversations in the past how to get started.

## I'm a content person. Do I really need to understand the technical parts?

If you typically work in a creative, editorial, marketing, or branding role, then dealing with modular content, metadata, logic, and relationships might feel foreign. How does this relate to communicating a message or telling a story? Do you need to know how to build databases and APIs?

No, probably not. But here's the thing: If you're the one who understands the content best, and who knows what readers and users want from it, then you're exactly the right person to be thinking about how it should be structured, stored, and transported—so you can keep its meaning and purpose intact. While this doesn't mean you need to become an XML expert, it does mean you should get more comfortable with the ideas presented in

Chapters 6 and 7, and be able to discuss needs, options, and priorities with those who will implement technical solutions.

## Is this just about mobile?

Yes and no. Getting content ready for mobile is a big challenge, and spawning all sorts of debate: Do we give mobile users just a portion of our content, allowing them to "snack"? Do we go responsive? Build an app? What does mobile mean, anyway: Is a tablet a mobile device, or something else? As these questions are raised, it becomes more and more clear that what we need is content that can go onto all the devices that exist now—and those that will exist in the future.

Smartphones may be disrupting our assumptions today, but they're just the beginning. TVs, household appliances, cars, and more are becoming Internet-enabled. Plus, there are content-shifting services like Instapaper and content-plucking sites like Pinterest to contend with, as I explore in Chapter 11. It would be easy to get overwhelmed, but the good news is this: The work you do now, to structure content for reuse and get it ready for mobile, is going to also make that content more prepared for wherever the future takes it.

# CONTENTS

How to Use This Book                    iv

Frequently Asked Questions              vi

Foreword                                xiv

Introduction                            xvi


**PART I: THE CASE FOR CONTENT EVERYWHERE**

**CHAPTER 1**

## Framing the New Content Challenge     3

More Content, More Work                  5

Making Content Work Harder               5

Getting Unstuck                          6

Thinking Beyond the Page                 8

Connecting the Dots                      10

Thinking Beyond the Website              11

Learning from Web Standards              12

You Can Start Today                      14


**CHAPTER 2**

## Building a Way Forward                 17

Tracing Our Lineage                      18

Putting the Pieces Together              22

Progress, Not Perfection                 24


**PART II: THE ELEMENTS OF CONTENT**

**CHAPTER 3**

## Breaking Content Down                  29

Deconstructing to Construct              30

First Meaning, Then Modeling             31

A Tale of Two Content Models             36

Enter, Content Strategy                  39

Common Content Types                     42

Turning Types into Elements 42

Not Just for Big Publishers 43

Structure Follows Substance 46

Coming Up for Air 47


**CHAPTER 4**

# Creating Content Models 51

Documenting a Content Model 52

Considerations and Compromises 56

CMS Capabilities and Trade-offs 61

Authors and Workflows 63

Turning Models into Ecosystems 73


**CHAPTER 5**

# Designing Content Systems 75

What Are Rules? 77

Why Rules Matter 79

A Framework for Rule-Making 88


**CHAPTER 6**

# Understanding Markup 95

Markup Matters 96

Many Meanings, Many Markups 96

What's Your CMS Got to Do with It? 98

The Semantics of…"Semantic" 99

The Lowdown on Markdown 104

Many Ways to Get to Markup 106

The Secret to Markup 107


**CHAPTER 7**

# Making Sense of Content APIs 109

What Is a Content API? 110

Content APIs in Practice 111

Why API? 115
API Approaches 115
Scoot Up to the API Table 117
Putting It All Together 117

## PART III: PUTTING STRUCTURED CONTENT TO WORK

**CHAPTER 8**

# Findable Content 121

More Structured, More Findable 122
Search Engine Findability 123
Site Search Findability 128
Smarter Faceted Search 129
Related and Contextually Discoverable Content 131
Curation: The Other C-Word 134
Finding Soul in Findability 134

**CHAPTER 9**

# Adaptable Content 137

Looking Beyond Layout 139
Intermixing Content 141
Content Layering 143
Removing Content 145
Making Content Lightweight 147
Simplicity from the Start 148
Adding Content 150
Responsibly Responsive 151

**CHAPTER 10**

# Reusable Content 153

Revisiting Content Reuse 154
Building a Central Content Store 155
Content Across Products 156

Personalized Content                                162
A Reuse Imperative                                  163
And Now for Something Completely Different          168
Chasing Perfection                                  170
Making Reuse Meaningful                             171

CHAPTER 11
**Transportable Content**                           **173**
The Great Content Shift                             175
What's in It for You?                               178
Taking Advantage of Content Shifting               179
More Portability, More Problems                     182
What You Can Do                                     185
Letting Go                                          186

PART IV: ENDURING CONTENT

CHAPTER 12
**Content and Change**                              **191**
Why You? Why Now?                                   192
Rethinking Content, Revealing Fracture             193
Making Change Stick                                 194
Building a Team                                     198
Being on the Outside                                199
Dealing with Fear                                   200
Putting People First                                200

CHAPTER 13
**Towards a New (Information) Architecture**        **203**
Designing for Change                                204
Architecture from Within                            205
The Problem with Mass Production                    207
Content in the Age of Mechanical Reproduction      208

Keeping the Aura Intact                                209
Content for Humans                                     210
The Road Ahead                                         210

**Index**                                              **213**
**Acknowledgments**                                    **222**
**About the Author**                                   **224**

# FOREWORD

When I decided to write *Content Strategy for the Web* in 2008, I knew with absolute certainty that I was not, in fact, a subject matter expert. I'd earned my undergraduate degree in theater, and my professional expertise lay primarily in making things up, depending what job I happened to have. Where did I get off thinking I could write a book about, well, *anything*?

What it came down to was this: I was a Web copywriter, and I was sick of the way people treated content as an afterthought. I wanted things to be different. And, ultimately, I had nothing to lose. No one knew who I was, so I had no literary reputation to uphold. Clearly no one cared about the topic, anyhow, so probably no one would read it. And it was with these extremely low expectations of myself that I began—and finished—the process of writing a book.

Then, just as one might hope, some people bought the book. Some conferences called and asked me to speak. And then, one morning I woke up to discover that, according to the Internet, I was suddenly a content strategy "subject matter expert," "thought leader," and "guru."

And that was when the imposter complex set in.

*\* \* \**

The imposter complex manifests like this. The more people tell you how smart you are—the more you hear about how your book is changing projects and companies and careers—the more you are absolutely convinced that any minute now someone is going to point a finger at you and say, "Waaaait a minute. YOU'RE not an expert! You're just someone who plays a content strategist on TV!" And then you will be exposed for the stupid, inexperienced jerk you are. Because clearly, *you* are not a subject matter expert. Only *real* experts write books. You should just stay home, eat toast, and keep quiet. You imposter.

*\* \* \**

In July of 2011, a relatively unknown content strategist named Sara Wachter-Boettcher posted the following statement to her brand-new blog: "I'm not a subject matter expert. But I play one on the Internet." She then proceeded to publish post after post about multiple facets of content strategy: editorial, user experience design, and content management. Her writing was smart, sassy, practical, and accessible.

After a while, Sara started digging into topics I had no experience with but was regularly asked to speak about. Intelligent content. Adaptive content. Structured content. While I understood these topics in a general, surface-y way, I was secretly terrified by them. I am not a technical person. I don't think in systems. I can't create or analyze complex CMS processes. But when Sara began to write about these topics, there was something about the way she approached them that made me feel, well, *smarter*. Like I understood not only what she was talking about, but why I should care about it in the first place.

And *that* is what a subject matter expert does.

\* \* \*

No matter where you are in your career, it's not easy to step up and say, "This is what I think. This is what I value. Here is why I think you should value it, too, and here is how we can do better work together." But if ever there were a time for content professionals to step up and share what they know—with each other, with their companies, and with clients—now is that time.

While we all continue to struggle with managing our website content, our other content problems are multiplying exponentially. Sara's book provides us with accessible, practical information that helps us navigate the current complexities of multichannel content. Moreover, it offers important alternatives to planning and structuring content that empower us to move confidently into the future, rather than constantly trying to recover from the past.

Sara has made her mark as a thought leader not because she was born that way, but because she has taken an enormously complex, intimidating topic and made it accessible to practitioners of all stripes. *Content Everywhere* promises to be the new bible for content professionals who are committed to creating meaningful content that can, at last, be free.

—Kristina Halvorson
Founder, Brain Traffic and Confab Events
Author, *Content Strategy for the Web*

# INTRODUCTION

There are people who've been structuring content in enterprise settings for more than a decade. I'm not one of them.

I didn't write this book because I have the most expertise in metadata, or because I've led the charge on building single-sourcing solutions for Fortune 500 companies. I wrote this book because I think there are lots of you out there like me: People who care about content, and who have invested countless hours in helping their organizations or clients communicate better, more consistently, more honestly. You've audited messy sites, rewritten robotic "about us" pages, restructured navigation, and thought long and hard about how to make things easy to find, read, and use.

And yet, if you're anything like me, you keep running into the same problem: Your content is stuck. It's not ready for mobile. It can't connect to other content on your site, much less elsewhere on the Web. It's fixed in pages and documents, siloed, and limited to a single access point. I felt like this for a long time. Working as a content strategist in a regional agency, I spent years trying my damnedest to clean up old content, get clients thinking about governance and maintenance, and improve the clarity and purposefulness of the content they were producing. Yet I was still hitting walls: mobile sites where content was left to rot because it was managed separately from the desktop version; "related content" modules that were largely irrelevant; clients who couldn't manage the content they had now but were certain they needed more, more, more.

Then, in the summer of 2011, I picked up *Responsive Web Design* by Ethan Marcotte. Knowing more about the Brazilian electroclash band CSS than cascading style sheets, I wasn't certain what would be in it for me. But as I learned about his technique for adapting layouts for different devices, it hit me: We can have all the technical know-how in the world, but our content's not ready for responsive design, nor for much of anything else the future might throw at it. Since then, I've been working on plenty of ideas for making content more future-friendly, flexible, and ready to travel, and this is the culmination of that work.

But this book is about more than creating a content strategy methodology for mobile. It's also about embracing a new mind-set—one focused on what content means and how it works, rather than where it lives and how it looks on any specific page. It's about breaking our reliance on old forms—fixed pages and documents—and replacing it with something that will hold up against a changing Web, and a changing world.

Most of all, this book is a start. I can't promise it will answer every question about the future of content. But I hope it gets you asking them.

# PART I

# The Case for Content Everywhere

Too often, today's content is fixed: stuck to individual pages or in device-specific applications. But as connected devices get more varied, robust, and ubiquitous—and as users expect to find, relate, and share content in more and more ways—we need content that can go anywhere, its meaning and message intact. So how do we stop making more content for every new device or channel and start doing more with the content we make? The answer starts with structuring our content for a future that's unfixed, fluid, and ever changing.

CHAPTER 1

# Framing the New Content Challenge

More Content, More Work       5

Making Content Work Harder       5

Getting Unstuck       6

Thinking Beyond the Page       8

Connecting the Dots       10

Thinking Beyond the Website       11

Learning from Web Standards       12

You Can Start Today       14

# S

arah Krznarich loves content.

As the assistant director of content strategy and student engagement for Arizona State University's Online campus from 2010 to 2012, her job revolved around keeping content fresh, smart, and useful.

When she joined the university, her job was pretty straightforward: She produced orientation content for students getting used to the ASU Online system. But those priorities shifted quickly when the school embarked on a website redesign in late 2010—a redesign that focused on publishing a wide range of content, as shown in Figure 1.1.

FIGURE 1.1
The redesigned homepage for ASU Online.

Eager to take ownership of the new site, Krznarich, a former magazine editor, listened intently as ASU Online's agency, Happy Cog, extolled the virtues of content strategy: the practice of understanding what content is needed to meet both users' needs and organizational goals, producing it, and creating realistic publishing and governance plans to keep it that way. She picked up *Content Strategy for the Web* by Kristina Halvorson. She read Ginny Redish's *Letting Go of the Words: Writing Web Content That Works.*

Armed with knowledge and backed by her passion for content, Krznarich jumped into action. She refined the ASU Online voice. She launched recurring features profiling current students. She started curating relevant news from outside sources. She pulled program descriptions from the main campus's assets and revised them for the Online campus's audience.

Krznarich was getting busy, and not in the recreational way. But the content was good, and the analytics were even better: In the first quarter after the site launched, information requests were up nearly 57 percent over the same period the prior year—and those visitors requesting information were doing so nearly a minute faster than before.

Total win, right?

## More Content, More Work

Yet Krznarich, now an independent content strategist, didn't quite see it that way. Whenever she wanted to update ASU Online's calendar, she had to find, copy, and paste relevant events from the main site. When a program was updated at ASU's main campus, she had to make a manual update on the Online site. Plus, there was the website for current ASU Online students, which featured similar, but more detailed, content as the site for prospects. When one required an update, the other was likely to need a refresh, too. And that was just the start.

It felt like the more content Krznarich made, the more she was asked to make content—and the less time she had to make it any *good*. But her content needs—and the time and resources it took to meet them? They kept on multiplying.

## Making Content Work Harder

Whether you've managed a website yourself or worked to architect, design, or build one, this plight may be familiar: content needs that grow and grow, siloed information that requires repetitive updates, and those who are responsible for it all left barely able to keep up.

Like ASU Online, maybe you've embraced the discipline of content strategy as a means to plan for and produce better content—content that's not just up-to-date, compelling, and meaningful, but also serves a purpose beyond filling space on a page. But investing in strategic, quality content takes time, skills, and money. Managing it takes even more. Even if you can allocate appropriate resources now, those resources will quickly be spread thin as devices and channels—and your need for quality content to serve them—continue to multiply.

What if there were a better way?

Instead of creating new content for every platform, channel, and device, what if people like Krznarich could put their valuable time and budget into better, more meaningful content assets, and do more with each one? What if there were a system for organizing and architecting content—one that actually made it easier for our organizations and clients to achieve a number of goals:

- Reuse content in multiple places and for multiple purposes.

- Make content more relevant and appropriate for users.

- Improve the experience of finding, using, sharing, and saving content across devices and channels.

- Spend less time managing content updates and maintenance.

- Still keep their message and editorial vision intact.

Turns out, there is. But it will take more than style guides and editorial calendars to get there.

If you want content that's ready for whatever the future holds, it's time to stop making more content, and instead start building systems that allow you to do more.

That's the mindset this book will help you embrace.

## Getting Unstuck

Let's start where our online content currently stops: namely, on the fixed webpages where most of it resides, unable to travel beyond the bounds of a single rendering—resulting in the broken experiences you see in Figure 1.2. Formatted through a content management system's WYSIWYG (what-you-see-is-what-you-get, or *whizzy-wig*) editor, most content today is designed to be displayed in just one way: on a desktop monitor. When viewed on devices with different screen sizes or capabilities, it quickly loses its hierarchy, priority, and organization.

FIGURE 1.2
Broken, blob-like,
inaccessible, or just plain ugly—
is this what we had in mind as our
content goes mobile?

Stripped from its format, content's meaning breaks down. Photos and captions that together tell a story become unrelated images and copy. Subheads become text snippets. Pull quotes become just another sentence in the endless flow of information. Systems to relate and link one piece of content with another are limited to manual tagging—time-intensive and prone to error—or traditional navigation systems, which tend to limit relationships to hierarchies.

In short, when we publish content while thinking solely about "pages," we end up with content that's fixed firmly to its place—far from the flexible and future-ready information we need.

Don't we want more for our content than this?

## Thinking Beyond the Page

I learned firsthand how limiting big, fixed pages of content could be while working on Arizona Office of Tourism's large state-run tourism website, arizonaguide.com. In 2009, as a newly minted content strategist working on a major overhaul of the site, I spent months auditing content, creating style and message guides, and editing key pages. I planned ahead, collaborated with the client's content creators and managers, and fought to have real content used in our designs. In short, I was living the content strategist's dream: plenty of messy content to work with, and clients who wanted me to make it better.

Only things didn't go quite as planned.

While I toiled away on Excel spreadsheets and governance guides, the rest of the team designed new features and built out templates. But at launch, a major problem emerged. Thousands of pieces of content about landmarks, businesses, and destinations existed in multiple unrelated legacy databases, each organized and labeled differently, making it impossible to create the relationships and context to transform them from disconnected data points into relevant content findable when and where it made sense.

Take the city of Sedona, shown in Figure 1.3. Famous for its stunning red rocks and artists' enclaves, it's chock-full of things to do, many of them the sort of once-in-a-lifetime activities travel magazines rave about: gorgeous hikes, posh spas, five-star golf resorts, even "energy vortices," if you're into that whole New Age thing.

FIGURE 1.3
Picture-perfect Sedona. Who *wouldn't* want to vacation here?

You wouldn't have known any of that information by looking at the city's page on the then-new website, a comp of which is shown in Figure 1.4. Featuring little but some canned copy and a link to Sedona's visitors' bureau, the page barely hinted at the plethora of things to do there. Perhaps worse, the content in the sidebar—including events, travel deals, and articles—was randomly selected on page load, not tied to Sedona at all.

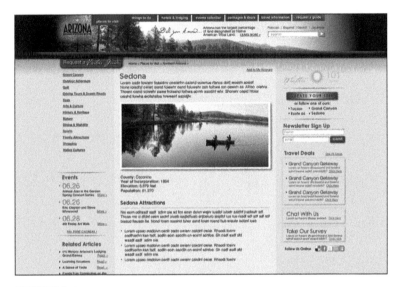

FIGURE 1.4
Sedona's page on the arizonaguide.com website.
Where'd all the magic go?

Want to visit Sedona? No problem. Want to learn about road biking tours? Easy. Want to see if anyone offers road biking tours *near Sedona?* Good luck.

The dots were all there, but there was no way to connect them. Between page-level content that lacked meaningful elements and outdated databases whose attributes were inconsistent or simply ignored, the site was missing a way to relate information across these disparate sections...even though that's exactly what our users wanted.

## Connecting the Dots

Thankfully, that's not where this story ends. It's actually where my own lean toward more flexible content begins, because I realized how little we could do with this high-quality but totally unstructured content.

A couple years later, I had the opportunity to begin solving the problem—and, more importantly, to help the Arizona Office of Tourism (AOT) staff understand that disconnected, fixed data was limiting their ability to create the experience they wanted, both for users with desktop computers and those on mobile devices.

As you'll see in detail later in this book, I did this by going back to those legacy databases, taking pages of content and identifying the salient pieces of information they're made of, then breaking those pages into content chunks to match. This allowed us to supplement our hierarchical site structure—that is, a standard navigation full of submenus—with a system based on shared content attributes, like the cities in which attractions were located, and logical rules that dictated how and when content should appear.

It's a work in progress, yes. Yet slowly but surely, their content is getting structured and stored in smarter ways, and thus becoming more capable of being reshaped and shifted for varying purposes. Just as critical, those who maintain the site are starting to think of their content as not just a series of pages, but an interconnected system of assets.

## Thinking Beyond the Website

While making content more flexible within AOT's site has been tremendously helpful, it's just the first step in their journey. Like most organizations, until recently, they managed just one website, designed around one screen size, and published across one channel.

But the way people access its content has shifted—and now we all need to bend with it.

According to a report from research firm StatCounter, mobile Internet usage, excluding tablets, has nearly doubled every year since 2009, and as of early 2012, it accounted for 8.5 percent of all Internet usage.[1] Meanwhile Cisco reports that by the end of 2012, there will be more mobile devices on earth than people.[2] And according to the Pew Research Institute, nearly half of American adults owned a smartphone as of February 2012, which was 11 percentage points higher than reported in Pew's prior survey, completed just nine months before, in May 2011.[3]

**TIP** DON'T BET ON ANY ONE DEVICE

Need to make the most of mobile? Be careful about locking your content into any one device. According to Cisco, by the time you read this, there are likely to be more phones on the planet than people—and with wildly varying forms and features.

---

1 http://rfld.me/PnMOvW

2 http://rfld.me/MxrAfU

3 http://rfld.me/OHTrN5

So the world's full of smartphones, but which kinds? Despite the venture capital thrown into iPhone apps, most of today's devices aren't brought to us by the letter *i*. In fact, during Q2 of 2012, 68 percent of the 158 million devices shipped globally used the Android platform, while just 16 percent were iOS-based.[4]

Then there are tablets and ereaders, which 29 percent of Americans reported owning by the start of 2012,[5]—not to mention the ultrabooks and countless other connected devices quickly hitting shelves with drastically different sizes and shapes.

Meanwhile, many organizations are managing much more than one online presence—such as Arizona State University and its multiple, independently managed websites—as well as sharing content across a wide range of social platforms.

Imagine jumping onto each of these bandwagons like the world jumped onto iPhone apps. Exhausting, right? As mobile strategist Luke Wroblewski writes in his book *Mobile First*, "Even if you can create native apps for each platform, the cost of maintaining them can quickly make it prohibitive."[6] After all, if your organization is already struggling to keep one website's content up to date, how will it fare when it's juggling a dozen different versions made for different devices?

## Learning from Web Standards

When you care about content, it's easy to become obsessed with displaying it *just so*: headlines perfectly sized to avoid awkward breaks, images flowing in-line with text at exactly the relevant part of the story, and quotations set off in a different color. But as I learned with my tourism client, perfect pages of content don't matter if users can't access them when they want them (or when you want them to).

The more you strive for the perfect page, the more you limit yourself to just that page. Instead, as you embrace more structured, reusable content, you can take some cues from folks on the design-and-development side of the universe, who blazed the trail of browser standards years ago by accepting that the obsession with pixel-perfect, identical design across browsers was unrealistic.

---

4  http://rfld.me/PIBXIY

5  http://rfld.me/NT2QAB

6  Luke Wroblewski, *Mobile First* (New York: A Book Apart, 2011).

Every time an improved browser version comes along or new internet device comes on the scene, it seems to break the site we just finished producing (or paying for). We build only to rebuild... merely to keep up with browsers and devices that seem determined to stay one budget-busting jump ahead of our planning and development cycles.

—Jeffrey Zeldman and Ethan Marcotte[7]

Today, the standards movement is leading to new approaches, like adaptive and responsive design, where a single site is designed with flexible grids and images, allowing it to resize and reflow on the fly to serve whatever display size you need—working beautifully on devices like smartphones, tablets, laptops, and desktops. Modes of thinking like "future friendly"—the work of Luke Wroblewski, Jason Grigsby, and a host of other prominent voices in mobile strategy and development—are spreading quickly, encouraging digital professionals to "acknowledge and embrace unpredictability."[8]

What unites these movements is a simple philosophy: That a website is inherently uncontrollable, and trying to reign it in—to give it the fixed precision that a printed page or physical canvas affords us—is an inherently losing battle. The only way to win is to let go of the exactitude of pixel perfection and embrace a more flexible set of standards and practices that ensure an accessible, usable experience for all. Even if, at times, the resulting display isn't as perfect as you'd like.

The same is true for content. As connected devices continue to multiply, and as users continue to expect to access your content in more and more places, the less you can afford to be rigid, manually applying content to each and every page. Instead, you need to create content in chunks, giving it the fluidity and flexibility for it to travel—across devices, sites, and channels—so users can experience it in whatever context they choose.

But content can't just be flexible; it must be meaningful as well. As your content becomes unfixed and free, it also needs standards that allow you to maintain its quality, message, and purpose so it retains those critical elements as it travels into the unknown.

---

7   *Designing with Web Standards,* Third Edition (Berkeley, California: New Riders, 2010).

8   Visit futurefriend.ly for the complete manifesto and a full list of participants.

## You Can Start Today

The Arizona Office of Tourism doesn't have the future all figured out. Despite all the improvements, the organization still operates a mobile site discrete from its main presence, using content from a separate database. Arizona State is trying, too, with initiatives like a new system that will allow event listings to be shared between the main campus and ASU Online—but the organization will still be updating program information manually for the foreseeable future.

Like those organizations, you may not have the tools, resources, or time to solve all your content problems today. That's OK. All you need is a commitment to thinking about content in a less fixed, more fluid way. After all, technological innovation isn't about to stop. Devices, platforms, and channels are only going to get more numerous and diverse. No one will be able to keep up with all of them.

This book isn't about keeping up. It's about creating a new framework: a mindset focused on designing for and building content that can have multiple purposes, and whose meaning can stay intact through multiple contexts. It's about structuring content so that it's flexible enough to fit the varied needs we have today, and strong enough to build on it with additional rules as they become necessary. It's not just about adapting to mobile, but also thinking about your content in more adaptable ways—ways that will help you both now and in the future.

It's about building a smarter, more sustainable way forward—and how we'll need to change our organizations to make that possible.

To do this, we need to draw on skills in content strategy, information architecture, and a host of other fields to get closer to content than ever before, understanding its inner workings and inherent meaning so that we can build the structures that support it.

This book will help you do just that by showing you how to:

- Identify content's meaning and elements at a micro level.
- Understand the relationships between content elements— and why they matter.
- Build content models that respect the complexity and message in your content.
- Start conversations about how you can store and mark up content in a future-friendly way.
- Allow your content to become unfixed and fluid.
- Begin considering what you can do with content as it is consumed on varied devices, channels, and even places outside your control.

With this framework in place, you can begin to set your content free, knowing it's ready for responsive designs, mobile devices, read-later apps, and a million other places it may go as this unfixed, flexible future continues to evolve. Your content will finally be fit to join the party—and you'll be confident it will represent you well, wherever it goes.

But there's still much work to be done. And it's going to take all of us to do it: content strategists, yes. But also information architects, user experience designers, developers, search engine marketers, writers, editors, new media publishers, and anyone whose role it is to create a digital space where content can exist and thrive—where audiences can find it, use it, learn from it, share it, and love it.

# CHAPTER 2

# Building a Way Forward

Tracing Our Lineage                                    18
Putting the Pieces Together                            22
Progress, Not Perfection                               24

F uture-ready, adaptable, flexible content requires a new framework, but take heart: You needn't start from scratch. Much of today's work has its origins in disciplines you likely already know a thing or two about. In this chapter, we'll explore those origins, creating a solid foundation upon which to build. We'll then take a look at how one organization is already putting the pieces together and creating a more flexible path for its content to travel.

With a look to the past and a bit of inspiration, you'll have your own starting point—a place from which you can roll up your sleeves and get to work.

## Tracing Our Lineage

This isn't the first time folks have talked about reusable content, meaningful messages, structured information, and designing systems that work harder. Instead, you can find the roots of today's movement in four key—and often overlapping—digital areas: content strategy, technical communications, information architecture, and content management.

### Content Strategy

If you work online, you work with content. Whether writing or filming it, coding or organizing it, labeling it or designing its typography, this work is all about creating a digital space where content can exist and thrive—and where it's findable, accessible, understandable, useful, and meaningful. Yet for years, that content was marginalized and ignored with the same refrains:

> "The site's all done. Now the client just needs to add content!"

> "Let's just launch now and fix it later."

> "It doesn't matter what it says. Just throw in some lorem ipsum."

These approaches resulted in little more than headaches and expensive delays, and as a result, websites often became a mess of disconnected, outdated, and useless content—content no one was responsible for, much less passionate about.

Enter content strategy: a discipline dedicated to reducing the pain of dealing with content that's gone wrong and determining viable plans for making it go right—for both users and organizations.

As Erin Kissane writes in *The Elements of Content Strategy*, content strategy sits somewhere between user experience, business analysis, marketing, publishing, and technical communications, and is an umbrella term for all work that:

- Helps companies understand and produce the kind of content their target audiences really need.

- Allows organizations to develop realistic, sustainable, and measurable publishing plans that keep their content on track in the long term.

- Cuts costs by reducing redundant or extraneous publishing efforts, while increasing the effectiveness of existing assets.

- Aligns communication across channels so that web content, print collateral, social media conversations, and internal knowledge management are working toward the same goals (in channel-appropriate ways).

- Prevents web projects from being derailed by the often major delays caused by underestimating the time and effort required to produce great content.[1]

Content strategy has caught on, and organizations far and wide have begun spending more time understanding their assets, articulating their goals, creating user-centered content, and improving the editorial quality of the things they produce.

But as digital spaces change, the approach to dealing with content must adapt as well. While message platforms and editorial guidelines will help, we also need to apply this passion for great content at a more systematic level. That's where today's work begins.

## Technical Communications

Systematic approaches are nothing new to folks in technical communications. Since at least the 1990s, technical writers and editors—those historically responsible for things like specification documents, instructions, and help guides—have been embracing ways of making content more structured and interconnected to meet the demands of publishing across large, distributed companies.

These pioneers developed ways to separate content's structure from its presentation, create repositories of content ready for reuse, and mark content up in a way that would allow it to travel between systems, resulting in

---

1   Erin Kissane, *The Elements of Content Strategy* (New York: A Book Apart, 2011).

approaches like DITA (Darwin Information Type Architecture), an XML-based language for authoring and publishing information in modules categorized according to topic.

Originally designed by IBM's technical communicators to help organize their own help documentation, DITA is perhaps best suited for marking up technical content, such as manuals for complex systems like military aircraft or computer hardware—use cases that don't always feel relevant to the wider world of digital professionals.

Moreover, this form of structured content can feel cold and clinical, especially to those from the editorial or marketing side of content, so it hasn't really caught on outside of very large enterprises managing vast amounts of technical data across distributed users.

It's hard to get people excited about XML, to be sure, especially when the rest of the team is talking about marketing campaigns and flashing design comps around. But, as we'll discuss more in Chapter 6, "Understanding Markup," the need to structure content and set it free now affects us all, working on all kinds of projects. And that means structure and markup need a fresh look, this time through the lens of meaning, form, and message—so content can go mobile, cross-channel, everywhere...all without losing its form and shape.

## Information Architecture

Systems, structures, and the shape of information—sound familiar? It should. Much of this new approach to content comes straight from good old information architecture, which Louis Rosenfeld and Peter Morville cemented as a critical interactive discipline in the late 1990s, and from which your own skills may well hail.

Often referred to as "the structural design of shared information environments,"[2] IA solidified as a practice to help solve several challenges parallel to those we face today. As the amount of information produced increased, information environments got more and more complex to support it. But they also became unwieldy, unusable, and impossible to manage. Information architects sought new ways of organizing and structuring all that data to facilitate users' access to and interaction with it.

As a discipline, IA defines spatial relationships and organizational systems, and seeks to establish hierarchies, taxonomies, vocabularies, and schema—resulting in documentation like sitemaps, wireframes, content types, and user flows, and allowing us to design things like navigation and search systems.

---

2  Peter Morville and Louis Rosenfeld, *Information Architecture for the World Wide Web*, Third Edition (Sebastopol, CA: O'Reilly, 2006).

The discipline of IA was also critical in establishing the use of content models—"'micro' information architectures made up of small chunks of interconnected data," as Morville and Rosenfeld called them, which we'll use at length in Chapter 3, "Breaking Content Down, and Chapter 4, "Creating Content Models."

A few years ago, content models were primarily used to support deep linking and related items within a single site—like connecting shoppers looking at a shirt with a listing for the matching pants. But today's challenge requires us to take our content models further, using them to guide and shape how content flexes to fit the demands of a cross-channel, multi-device universe.

As content continues to get easier to produce, more interrelated, and less fixed to its original place of publication, we must focus more energy than ever on defining these micro information systems, establishing architectures that tackle the messier world of our content's meaning—something we'll do throughout this book.

As we do this, we'll need to create experiences that are not just hierarchical or linear, but flexible, modular, relational, and semantic. Which means if you already have IA skills, you're needed now more than ever.

## Content Management

Ask any organization's website manager or communications specialist about her CMS and you're likely to get a sigh, a four-letter word, or—perhaps worst of all—a shrug of the shoulders and a look of resignation.

Content management systems don't have the best reputation, but there's still plenty we can learn from them—and plenty we can do to improve them. Because, in actuality, the problems with mobile and the problems with our CMSs are actually the same, as leading mobile and content strategy advocate Karen McGrane says:

> If we're going to succeed in publishing content onto a million different new devices and formats and platforms, we need interfaces that will help guide content creators on how to write and structure their content for reuse.[3]

Designed to streamline routine website updates and create a publishing platform less-technical staff can understand, CMSs do make some things easier for organizations. But they also cause their own set of problems. Editors and writers find them hard to use. Those WYSIWYG editors let well-meaning contributors turn perfectly good text into pink, bolded nightmares. Sites are typically arranged in strict hierarchies, not

---

3  http://rfld.me/PkiBxx

relationships—resulting in endless disconnected pages, not modules or systems that can be related and remixed.

Perhaps worst of all, content management systems are often unfriendly to their end users: the authors publishing in them. And they're not sold or implemented in a way to help the authors get tasks done efficiently and effectively.

Today, however, folks are starting to address this problem by focusing on "author experience," which is the flipside to user experience. Just as basic UX principles tell us to help users achieve tasks without frustration or confusion, author experience design focuses on the tasks and goals that CMS users need to meet—and seeks to make it efficient, intuitive, and even pleasurable for them to do so.

Put this way, it seems so obvious: *of course* the people creating and managing content are users, too. But in reality, today's CMSs often seem to challenge users as much as they help. And as we all know, a frustrated user will abandon the process, avoid the system, or end up with errors.

Poor author experience can be just as detrimental. When CMS authors are frustrated or confused, they make errors or simply don't bother to complete tasks fully—choosing, for example, to leave fields blank rather than navigate a painful series of drop-down menus. As a result, content creation takes longer than it ought, yet still winds up inaccurate and inflexible...*and* your workforce becomes frustrated and either unable or unwilling to care about your users.

As we'll discuss in detail in Chapter 4, we now have the chance to stop creating such lose-lose situations and start incorporating content creators and strategists—those who know the content best—into the CMS selection, customization, and implementation process. When we do, we can develop CMSs that are both user-friendly and ready for the structure, rules, and relationships needed for content to travel across devices and channels.

## Putting the Pieces Together

Whew. So you have a foundation and some skills to help along the way. But it's always easier to get started with an example to guide you. Before you dig into your own content, let's look at how one organization has stopped the endless cycle of more content for more places and started designing systems that let its content go further.

National Public Radio, the United States' public- and donor-funded multimedia organization, has become the poster child for major media getting more flexible with content, seeing its overall page views increase by 80 percent in 2010 alone and attributing the bulk of that increase to its mobile efforts. But it wasn't always this way.

Back in 2007, when Zach Brand joined NPR to head up its technology efforts for digital media, he started talking with the organization's member stations—all those affiliate radio stations that carry NPR programming in their local markets—and seeing what their experiences and challenges were. By and large, they told him their websites were the problem—or more specifically, their sites' content.

While NPR is known for radio programming that features detailed storytelling, in-depth interviews, and investigative reporting, none of that content was reaching its member stations' sites. Instead, NPR was providing just short news briefs. Though informational and newsworthy, these stories lacked the depth and emotional connection NPR fans had come to expect—and that NPR held as the core of its content strategy.

This need to provide member stations with rich, satisfying content was at the heart of NPR's decision to build a system for more flexible content—content that would support their strategic goals, anywhere it went.

First, the team revisited its information architecture, defining the types of content NPR produces and building a structure that supported them. Then it revisited the CMS, improving its interfaces for all that newly restructured content, as well as helping reporters and editors understand how all this would enable them to produce better stories. Finally, NPR built an API—an application programming interface, which we'll discuss more in Chapter 7, "Making Sense of Content APIs,"—which opened its content up for use by other websites, making that content more reusable and reconfigurable.

With its API in place, NPR quickly began seeing more opportunities for its content—this time, looking inward. Rather than focusing on how others are using NPR content, the organization is now enhancing how it uses its own content, putting its API to work for multiple platforms and products, like NPR Music, the NPR News iPhone app, and NPR's listings in iTunes.

It calls this approach, quite aptly, COPE: Create Once, Publish Everywhere. The concept is simple: create one set of content affiliated with each story, enter it into a CMS with structured attributes, and allow that same content—made available via the NPR API—to be accessed by both member stations and NPR's own suite of products.[4] Just a few of these outputs are shown in Figure 2.1.

---

4   Karen McGrane has done an excellent job describing COPE in her talk, "Adapting Ourselves to Adaptive Content," available on Slideshare at http://rfld.me/Nx5Kbl.

NPR.ORG     NPR iPAD APP     WBUR.ORG     M.NPR.ORG  IPHONE APP

FIGURE 2.1

NPR's COPE model gets content onto multiple NPR websites and mobile products, as well as to its member stations.

As you'll see more of in Chapter 3, this approach has had a number of benefits for NPR and its member stations, including better content in more places, less duplication of editorial efforts, higher consistency, more control over quality, and easier story updates.

That doesn't mean it's perfect. For example, it's primarily been a one-way system so far. While it's great for sending its own content out across platforms, as of this writing, NPR is just starting to toy with ways to receive content from external sources—so NPR's member stations can't easily send their features back up the chain to the national office.

Imperfect as it is, COPE is helping NPR...well, *cope* with a rapidly changing publishing landscape. It puts the organization squarely ahead of most others when it comes to mobile, and in some ways, that's no surprise. After all, at NPR, content *is* the product, and every member of the organization understands its importance, including techy types like Zach Brand. With a large content-producing staff and plenty of editors, setting an editorial vision and publishing workflow isn't new there. Plus, NPR has been sharing content with member stations since the 1970s, so while its delivery method may have shifted from satellite to API, it's been packaging stories for broader consumption for four decades.

## Progress, Not Perfection

Not a major media outlet whose product is content? That's OK. Rather than relying on technologists to start looking at content more closely, it's up to you to take the first step, even if you can't tackle all your content challenges at once.

Whatever your background—content strategist or manager, technical communicator, information architect, writer, editor, or any other role that gets into the thick of the content—it's up to you to break out of your professional comfort zone, glean some skills from all the disciplines we've talked about here, and collaborate on a better way forward.

By breaking content down into components and understanding how a piece of content comes to mean what it does, you can begin to make more informed decisions about how you build, organize, and use it—decisions that will allow you to bring a new content framework to technical teams and ultimately create experiences with the longevity to serve users and organizations far beyond a single page.

Part II of this book, "The Elements of Content," is where we'll do just that. In Chapter 3, "Breaking Content Down," you'll learn how to analyze a piece of content, breaking it down into its building blocks and documenting the micro structures within that make it whole.

In Chapter 4, "Creating Content Models," you'll take that intimate knowledge of your content and use it to create rich, useful content models—models that support your content's meaning and make your databases and content management systems smarter. We'll also talk about how to better collaborate with the technical teams typically tasked with this process, as well as how to implement content models in a way that respects writers' and editors' skill sets, time, and priorities.

With smarter attributes and more reusable content "chunks" planned, Chapter 5, "Designing Content Systems," will show you how to think through the logic and business rules and conditions that will define how your content is used, combined, and displayed across experiences.

In Chapter 6, "Understanding Markup," you'll see how content can be prepared for transport with an overview of some current and emerging markup technologies used to keep structures intact as content travels. Finally, we'll complete our methodology in Chapter 7, "Making Sense of Content APIs," by discussing content-focused APIs and their role in getting content everywhere it needs to go.

Part III of this book, "Putting Structured Content to Work," will explore how you can put smart, structured content to work, and the benefits you'll reap when you do. It starts with Chapter 8, "Findable Content," which explores using structure to improve navigation, related and contextual systems, site search, and SEO.

In Chapter 9, "Adaptable Content," we'll explore how your understanding of content types, as well as their inherent relationships and priorities, can help you make decisions about how that content should flex for different displays, such as in a responsive or adaptive website.

Chapter 10, "Reusable Content," will show you how to put content modeling to work to repurpose content in a variety of ways, looking at examples of centralized content stores, personalized content, and more from technical communications, government, and major retailers.

As your content travels, unfixed from a single site, you must learn to let it go. In Chapter 11, "Transportable Content," we'll do this by discussing how content is shifting away from sites and into users' control. We'll also see how structure can give you a better foundation for saving and sharing, and possibly help you retain authorship information and data about content circulation in the future.

Part IV of this book, "Enduring Content"—which includes Chapter 12, "Content and Change," and Chapter 13, "Towards a New (Information) Architecture"—will leave you with a mindset that will help you prepare both your content *and* your organization for a more flexible, less fixed future.

There's no time to waste. Let's go.

# PART II

# The Elements of Content

Before your content is ready to travel, you need to understand what it is—and not just at the surface level. Let's now dive into the depths of your content, breaking it down into meaningful dimensions and asking tough questions along the way. As a result, you'll have the tools to structure content in more useful ways, communicate your content models to others, and prepare for publication across platforms and devices—all while keeping your content's message, and its purpose, firmly intact.

# CHAPTER 3

# Breaking Content Down

Deconstructing to Construct 30

First Meaning, Then Modeling 31

A Tale of Two Content Models 36

Enter, Content Strategy 39

Common Content Types 42

Turning Types into Elements 42

Not Just for Big Publishers 43

Structure Follows Substance 46

Coming Up for Air 47

The challenge of making content more flexible begins with its name: content. Vague and expansive, the term alone does little to explain itself—and makes it easy to assume that any one piece of it is the same as another. But as anyone who's worked with just a bit of content knows, there's quite a variety that can exist within those seven little letters. From 140-character Tweets to 10,000-word articles, video clips to thumbnail images, all kinds of things can fall into this big, bursting content bucket.

In order to set your content free from the limitations of generic pages, you need to get much more specific about what that content is—understanding its meaningful dimensions and its inherent form—so you can ensure the way you structure and store it makes sense.

In this chapter, we'll do the prep work for content modeling by taking a deep dive into our content's meaning, then:

- Learning about content models.

- Analyzing content types, purposes, and goals.

- Assessing the content elements you have—or need—to meet your goals.

Together, this in-depth knowledge will allow you to identify the priorities, relationships, and dependencies that will guide how you ultimately document your models and modularize your content, which we'll work on in Chapters 4, "Creating Content Models, and 5, "Designing Content Systems."

## Deconstructing to Construct

If you're new to content modeling, think of it like this: It's the process of first understanding the *concept* of a specific type of content—how your users perceive and understand the various pieces and parts it comprises—and then creating a *structure* that supports those components and relationships. By modeling, you create a tangible representation of the content that will serve as your guide as you write, edit, design templates, configure content management systems, and more.

Why do all this? Well, content modeling is the first step toward winning the war between "blobs versus chunks," as Karen McGrane calls them—between content that's shapeless and fixed and content that's modular and flexible. In other words, you can't have content everywhere unless you start with a smart model.

Breaking content down into its logical parts also provides practical benefits right on a single site, including:

- Allowing you to move forward with website and CMS specifications before all the content is complete, because you know what each template should be able to support.

- Giving those tasked with collecting, writing, and editing content a clear list of items to create or assemble.

- Providing user experience and interface designers with concrete elements to incorporate in their wireframes and comps. Most of all, content modeling gives you systemic knowledge; it allows you to see what types of content you have, which elements they include, and how they can operate in a standardized way—so you can work with archetypes, rather than designing each one individually.

> **NOTE** **MODELS AND TYPES AND ELEMENTS, OH MY!**
>
> Before we get too deep, let's define some terms. The terminology out there may vary, but in this book, I refer to a *content type* as the actual thing a user would read or use, like an article, a recipe, or a help guide entry. Meanwhile, *content elements* are the modules and chunks that make up that content type: ingredients, summaries, teasers, and the like. A *content model* is the connective tissue between all of them—the expression of how all those types and elements coexist. You can make models of individual content types that show how each chunk of content comes together, which we'll do next, as well as models of entire content systems, which show how multiple content types are interconnected based on rules and relationships, which we'll start to tackle in Chapter 5.

A content model typically ends up being documented in a diagram that can get translated to a database and CMS structure. But we're not quite ready to build a model yet. First, we'll spend this chapter learning how to deconstruct content along meaningful lines that make sense to users and also map to organizational goals and strategies. Only then will we be ready to document our models and get them implemented.

# First Meaning, Then Modeling

Content modeling isn't unique to today's mobile, multichannel world. Many IAs have been doing it for years, as have technical communicators, database developers, CMS vendors, and even a content or metadata specialist or two.

The difference is, these efforts often focused more on data storage and retrieval than on the content itself. So today, we're not going to dive right into making diagrams and specs. Instead, we're going to spend some time thinking about meaning *before* we get to modeling. Why? Because while it takes a little bit of technical know-how to implement a model, content can be ambiguous—which means that the art of modeling must start long before the spreadsheets and data tables come out.

As content strategist R. Stephen Gracey puts it, "content modeling is more than fields":

> We find ourselves pushed into the thick of technical specification before we've had a chance to imagine what the content is supposed to *be* and *do*, let alone how it should be *structured*.
>
> In my view, we'd be nearer the truth of "modeling" if we took our cues from other disciplines... The sculptor "models" in clay before casting in bronze... The industrial designer creates digital "models" before production... Content must be modeled in this *creative* sense, as well as in the *technical* sense.[1]

In other words, arbitrarily chunking content into parts gives us a model, but it doesn't necessarily make it a meaningful one. Shaping the right model in the first place takes work.

Naturally, I learned this the hard way, as many of us who got into digital work without formal training did. A few years ago, I worked on a project for a large international brand where we were adding retail locations to one of the company's many sites. Someone from the corporate office sent over a CSV file of location data. It was handed straight to the development team, and the fields in that file immediately became the fields in the CMS template (shown in Figure 3.1) without anyone giving it a moment's thought.

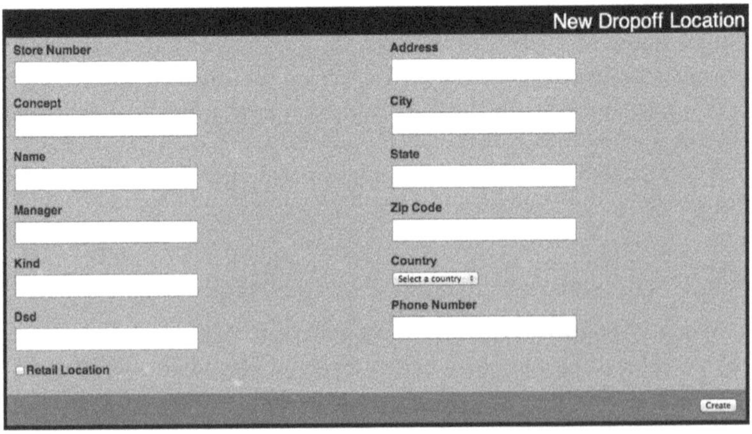

FIGURE 3.1
Dsd? Kind? When you consider your content's purpose when making database decisions, you can avoid poor labeling and useless fields like these.

---

1  http://rfld.me/MQHbvB

Between indecipherable labels like "Dsd" and open-entry fields labeled "Kind"—kind of *what*, exactly?—half the fields were either unintelligible or unnecessary. As a result, those responsible for content governance had no idea how to manage these listings effectively.

Fifteen minutes spent thinking about the content within that spreadsheet *before* the CMS template was built would have solved this problem. But the developer imported what he was given, and that was that.

**TIP** ADAPTING YOUR PROCESS

How does this close reading of your content fit into your project—*and* your process? Typically, the earlier you start assessing your content, the more chance you'll have to use that knowledge later, influencing everything from sitemaps to faceted search and sort features to CMS requirements to content production.

Written down like this, the scenario sounds almost silly. Who let this happen? But in truth, content ends up being modeled like this all the time, in organizations large and small. Maybe even in your own.

We can do better than this, but only when we begin to understand which core elements make our content types come to life—and then share that knowledge with the folks building the physical systems and structures that will support our lively, user-satisfying content.

As content management expert Deane Barker has written, "structuring content can suck the soul out of the authoring process"[2] by making those responsible for content stop thinking in wholes and start acting like machines. That's probably true, but it needn't be. If those of us who care about delivering great content and experience—like writers, editors, UXers, strategists, and designers—take the lead on making content models that are rich and meaningful, then we won't have to choose between structure and soul.

Sound good? Then it's time to get to work by exploring your content more closely than ever and getting at the center of what makes it tick.

---

2  http://rfld.me/NT31f3

*If you think breaking content down and considering its parts seems mundane, you haven't talked with R. Stephen Gracey. A long-standing proponent of content modeling, he has plenty of advice for finding the beauty in this often mechanical-seeming process, and he agreed to share just a bit of it with us.*

**You talk about content modeling as art. Why? What artistic skills apply here?**

Any creative endeavor has two parts, the art and the craft. To embark on the study of an art, we start with a disciplined study of the craft. This study involves five components: experience, instruction, experimentation, practice, and above all, enjoyment.

We *experience* the art we are learning. Writers read voraciously. Musicians listen constantly. We build a cumulative familiarity, conscious and unconscious, with the art's forms, ideas, intentions, vocabulary, history, and more. We also receive *instruction*, whether from books or people. We learn "about" the art and see how techniques and approaches result in a finished product.

We *experiment*. We imitate and emulate. We sketch. We take things apart. We refine our efforts and discover new avenues to explore. Curiosity leads us more deeply into the art. We also *practice*, honing our skills through endless repetition. And finally, all this is fueled by *enjoyment*. Not all the steps are fun all the time, but you must derive fulfillment and meaning from the craft. It is through the mastery of the craft that the art emerges.

Being artistic about content modeling requires all these things. It's a continual search for examples of content to understand how things work or don't work, conversations with other practitioners to learn from them and also to teach. We must sketch and rework our models, fill them with real content and see how they do. And of course, we just need to learn to enjoy the process of getting inside the content and building new forms, and find fulfillment in producing an integrated, living whole.

### What about the content itself? How does it stay alive as you break it apart?

Modeling is the study of some real object, so that it can be represented in another medium. For example, "sketching" is primarily a technique for discovering an object's underlying structure. You "see" better when you sketch. You become aware of the elements that make up your subject, so that when they "create" the art, you already understand what holds it together—what to put in, and what to leave out. It works for writers, too. Outlining helps you find the boundaries of your subject and sort out which ideas should be included or excluded.

Painters, composers, writers, and designers all learn that they must be able to work on the pieces of a composition, while at the same time standing back to see how the composition "works" as a whole. Content modeling is the same. You must be able to consider both the underlying structure of the content and the "gestalt"—the shape or form—of the overall effect. Done well, the viewer doesn't focus on those parts, but is left only with the sense that the composition "lives."

### How should someone get started thinking about content's structure?

Your goal cannot be to have as few content types as possible, with as few fields as possible. A system with only one content type is like a site with only one navigation link, labeled "Everything." Once you've accepted that a good system has "just the right number" of content types, the way is clear to be expansive in discovering how many types there might be.

Like any good brainstorming technique, the discovery of content types should begin broadly, not thinking about how many templates you'll have to create, not worrying about the connections among the types, and not limiting by size or other properties. There will be plenty of opportunity to narrow down and "be realistic" later in the process.

*See what else Gracey is thinking about at his blog,* contentstrategy.rsgracey.com.

# A Tale of Two Content Models

To understand why close evaluation of content is so critical for modeling, let's take a look at a content type you've likely seen and perhaps even worked with: a recipe.

Which content elements does a recipe need? If you said title, ingredients, and directions, that's a start. But oftentimes, there may be much more to it.

I learned this while working on a website overhaul for a quickly growing grocery company. With hundreds of locations and a focus on fresh, natural products, the chain had a large following of fans interested in healthy eating and specialty diets like vegan and gluten-free, as well as a repository of recipes that had been previously published in its email newsletters. To meet the goals of engaging site visitors and reinforcing the chain's fast, fresh, and healthy brand messages—while driving fans to buy more products, of course—we decided to publish relevant recipes alongside product pages across the site.

As we began scratching the surface, we saw a whole universe of elements contributing to this content's meaning and helping us toward our goals. This led us to build a content model (shown in Figure 3.2) that included not just the basics like ingredients, directions, and yield, but also:

- **Teasers** to provide context and drive interest when displayed throughout the site.

- **Nutritional information** to support the brand's health-conscious appeal.

- **Specialty tags,** like vegan or gluten-free, to assist those with dietary restrictions.

- **Cooking and prep time** data to reinforce the idea that healthy, home-cooked meals don't need to be hard.

- **Categories** that mapped back to the brick-and-mortar stores' layout, allowing site visitors to easily know where to shop for ingredients when in the store, while also allowing the chain to display more relevant supplemental content to people visiting those sections of the website.

FIGURE 3.2
A grocery chain's recipe content model, where content elements match the store's fast, fresh, and healthy branding.

These content attributes aren't the only meaningful dimensions you could glean from a recipe, however. For a different perspective, let's look at another approach to the same type of content: the recipe model used by Epicurious, as seen in this top-rated pizza recipe shown in Figure 3.3.

FIGURE 3.3

A recipe for some tasty-looking goat cheese pizza from Epicurious.com.

While we can't speak to Epicurious' specific business goals, we can make some reasonable assumptions. First, the site is owned by Condé Nast. As a publisher that runs extensive banner advertising, Epicurious likely wants to increase page views in order to bolster ad revenue, and get recipe hunters to view content on or subscribe to its other food-related media properties, like *Bon Appétit*—very different goals than our grocery friends, and aims that have led Epicurious to use a long list of content elements, as shown in Figure 3.4:

- Title
- Byline
- Publication attribution
- Yield
- Active time
- Total time
- Teaser description
- Image
- Ingredients
- Preparation
- Wine pairings
- Reviews
- Main ingredients
- Type
- Dietary considerations
- Related menus
- Related recipes

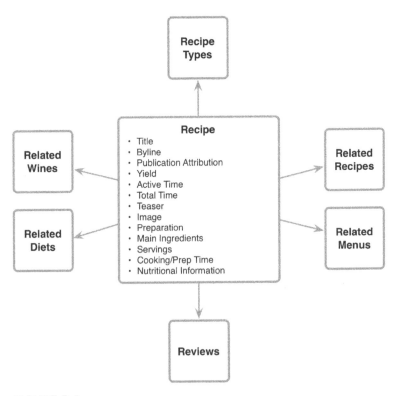

FIGURE 3.4
What Epicurious' recipe content model appears to look like. Note that it's both more detailed and just plain different than the model in Figure 3.2.

Two recipes, two very different content models—each seemingly complete. So how do you figure out the right one for your content? What level of detail do you need? To answer that question, we need to take a step back and determine what you're trying to accomplish in the first place.

## Enter, Content Strategy

Content modeling requires you to simultaneously understand your goals at the highest level *and* get intimate with your content's most minute attributes, and there's a pretty big chasm in between. Luckily, there's an entire discipline dedicated to bridging that divide: content strategy.

At its most basic, a content strategy outlines how content will be used to support both overall organizational goals and audiences' needs. While there are many approaches to articulating a content strategy and a million ways to customize one for a specific project or problem, it should at a minimum include several items:

- **Goals:** How will content support your overall strategy? What should it accomplish for your organization? For your users?

- **Resources:** How much time and money do you have for your content? What skill sets are on hand?

- **Key messages:** What are the top organizational messages you want content to communicate? What do your users need?

- **Voice and tone:** How does your brand translate to your online presence? What should you sound like?

If you're new to content strategy, and don't foresee your project benefiting from a dedicated content strategist anytime soon, I highly suggest you spend a little extra time figuring this part out.[3] It will serve you well as we travel the long road into the future, because each decision you make about content—what you publish, how it's structured, and where it goes—will come out of this strategy.

Once you understand (and get the team to agree on) what content is intended to do for your organization, you're ready to start evaluating the types of content you have against those goals. In other words, you'll now take your macro content strategy, which may affect the entire organization, and apply it, piece by piece, to each of the content types you have.

One of the best ways to begin this process is with a content audit—an in-depth accounting of all the content that exists.

---

3  To get started with content strategy, pick up Kristina Halvorson and Melissa Rach's *Content Strategy for the Web*, Second Edition (Berkeley, California: New Riders, 2012) or Erin Kissane's *The Elements of Content Strategy* (New York: A Book Apart, 2011).

Content audits, like the excerpt shown in Figure 3.5, are useful for all kinds of things, but at their most basic, they outline what content you already have and where it can be found. They come in all shapes and sizes, from qualitative evaluations that look for outdated, off-brand, or ineffective content to quantitative reviews of all assets to make sure nothing is missing before defining a new taxonomy for a website.[4]

**Content Audit**
www.sarawb.com
10 12

SWB

| Quantitative Metrics | | | | | | Qualitative Metrics | | | | |
|---|---|---|---|---|---|---|---|---|---|---|
| Page Name | URL | Content Type | Page Purpose/Goal | Content Elements | Length | Complete? | Useful? | On Brand? | Voice / Style? | Notes |
| Homepage | www.sarawb.com | Homepage | Communicate who I am, credibility, and experience immediately. | Introductory copy, image, recent blog post snippets, recent project snippets, footer with Twitter, subscribe, and get in touch. | 150 words | 3 | 4 | 5 | 5 | Refresh to show recent consulting work. |
| About | http://sarawb.com/about/ | Content Page | Provide detail on experience and personality. | Multiple paragraphs of text, image of Sara, bullet points about experience. | 300 words | | | | | |
| Contact | http://sarawb.com/contact-me/ | Contact Form | Allow those interested in working with me a way to get in touch. | Short blurb, contact form with simple fields. | | | | | | |
| Blog | http://sarawb.com/blog/ | Recent Posts | Showcase insight and expertise by tackling hot topics. | | | | | | | |
| This time with feeling: A fresh look at content modeling | http://sarawb.com/2012/04/23/content-modeling/ | Blog Post | Detailed look at a topic relevant to upcoming book. | | | | | | | |
| Responsive-Ready Content | http://sarawb.com/2012/03/07/content-strategy-responsive-design/ | Blog Post | | | | | | | | |

FIGURE 3.5
Content audits, like this excerpt, needn't be pretty. They just need to document what you have, where it is, and any other information relevant to your project.

When it comes to defining meaningful dimensions for your content structures, though, your top priority during the audit phase is to understand the types of content that exist currently—and how consistent their attributes are.

But content types are more than just labels like "articles" or "blog posts"; they're an exploration of the content's purpose: What role does it play in achieving your goals? For each distinct purpose you can unravel, you likely have a discrete content type.

To start this process, analyze your content against the following questions:

- Which of your content goals does this type of content support? How? For example, my grocery client wanted to be seen as healthy, so including healthy recipes with prominent nutritional information was important.

4 If you're new to content auditing, don't miss Chapter 5 of Halvorson and Rach's book.

- Why would a user want this content? What does it achieve for her? Customer research told this grocery store that shoppers tended to be "assemblers," not chefs—folks who want to eat fresh, homemade meals without a ton of work. Therefore, recipes needed to show how their products could be used in tasty, easy-to-prepare ways.

- What do you want users to do once they've consumed this content? For some organizations, this is easy—after all, "buy more groceries" was an obvious goal for my grocery client. But you might find others that are subtler, such as those relating to education, brand loyalty, or simply understanding.

The level of granularity you'll need in your content types depends on your organization's industry and goals. Take the term "article." With my grocery client, this was a specific enough type, because all articles served the same singular purpose. Whether it was a video showcasing where a fair-trade coffee supplier obtained its beans or a detailed guide to which apples were best for what, every article was designed to demonstrate the brand's commitment to healthy, natural—yet tasty—foods, and to build deeper connections between shoppers and the products they bought.

But what if you're working with a media company, like a magazine or news site? Here, the term "article" is uselessly vague: Does it mean features? Editorials? Columns? News briefs? All of the above? These types of content likely accomplish very different things for a publication and for its readers or subscribers. Treating them as a single content type, then, won't give you the flexibility you need.

In addition to documenting which content types you have, you can also use this moment to analyze whether there are additional types you need. Go back to your overall content goals and ask: Do we have content that is reaching each of these effectively? What's missing? What about for our users? Have we done enough user research to know what they want, and whether they're getting it? What new types of content would help fill the gaps?

Just as critical, now's the time to note any content that seems extraneous. Are there items you simply don't need? If there's no organizational or user goal being met by an entire type of content, it's just clutter. Unfixing it from a page to travel freely across multiple sites and experiences will only further muck things up—for your brand and for the people who encounter it. Cut it now, before it does additional harm.

Once done with your audit, you should have a clear sense of how many types of content you have, and how they're different from one another—a great starting point for structuring and modeling that content in better, more useful ways.

# Common Content Types

So what does a content type actually look like? While your findings will vary, some common examples include:

- Bios
- Blog posts
- Business listings
- Episodes
- Event listings
- Fact sheets
- FAQs

- Feature articles
- Help/user assistance modules
- Podcasts
- Poems
- Press releases
- Products

- Recipes
- Reviews
- Short stories
- Testimonials
- Tips and lists
- Tutorials

This list could go on and on, and vary greatly by industry. Point is, get to know what you're dealing with, and why it's important. Because you'll need this knowledge in order to make smart, useful decisions about how you define its elements, store it, mark it up, and—ultimately—let it travel into an unknown future across varied devices and channels.

It's important to note that I've left user interface copy, also called microcopy or in-line help, out of this list on purpose. That's because here, we're focused on the content that takes center stage: the information the site showcases, not the bits of content used to guide people to and around it. Moreover, you'll likely always need different interface copy for different purposes. But don't be fooled: UI copy is, indeed, important stuff—and will need careful attention as well.[5]

# Turning Types into Elements

Establishing your content types sets the stage for the next step in breaking your content down: identifying the dimensions of each one. To do this, you need to know which elements exist in a given type of content, and whether they're complete. A good way to start this process is to evaluate your content through a user's perspective first: What do they see, and how do they perceive the information? How would you present the content to ease their understanding? Are there obvious distinctions between parts of content, such as titles, teasers or copy decks, subheads, lists, pull quotes, images, captions, or related items?

---

5 For help making microcopy work, see "Micro Copy: Content Strategy and Writing the User Interface" from Amy Thibodeau at http://rfld.me/QbOH3u.

The specific elements you'll uncover will vary, depending on the type of content you're working with. But regardless of what you find, content elements should always accomplish two things:

- **Be distinct from one another.** A content element can (and likely will) be related to and dependent on other elements, but it should also be distinct from those elements. If breaking content into two elements feels forced, you may be trying to chunk information that's best left in one piece.

- **Represent a unit of information.** Each content element won't tell a complete story—that's why they're just chunks, not narrative wholes. But it should always contain enough information to communicate something specific, such as a summary, quote, or list.

Take our example from Chapter 2, "Building a Way Forward." As NPR began working through the COPE model—that's "Create Once, Publish Everywhere," for those who've been skimming—the team had some decisions to make about how, precisely, this freewheeling, flexible content they envisioned would be created and organized within their CMS.

When NPR started considering this, the first question was, "What's our basic building block?" says Zach Brand, NPR's head of technology—in other words, what brought their content to life?

Initially, the team thought it was *shows*—the NPR programs like "All Things Considered" or "Talk of the Nation" that you'd traditionally hear on the radio. But after scratching a bit deeper, they discovered that the real kernel of NPR content was the *story*.

So what makes a story at NPR? Well, that all depends on the story. Some have rich visual and audio assets, some don't. Some are long, some short. But, says Brand, at their core, all stories include a minimum of four key attributes: a headline, a teaser blurb, a longer description, and a date stamp. Everything else is optional, and depends on what the editor has available, what's most relevant to the topic, and where it will be used.

## Not Just for Big Publishers

It's not surprising that an organization like NPR—one that has been working with complex content for decades, and that has always packaged its stories and made them available for its member stations' platforms—has a leg up when it comes to creating editorially driven content elements designed for reuse.

Most of your companies and clients probably aren't major media organizations with large editorial staffs. If your project isn't as sophisticated as NPR, don't worry: There's still plenty you can do simply by honing a keen editorial eye.

Just as we broke down Epicurious' recipe into more than a dozen parts, a close reading of just about any content type will reveal multiple distinct elements. Here are a few of the ones I've found most common:

- **Title/headline:** This is a given for most content. Typically just a few words long, though not always, the title is the most common entry point to the content.

- **Copy deck/teaser/synopsis:** These little tidbits may go by various names, but their structure is typically similar: short, punchy copy that leads users into the content.

- **Attribution/byline:** Content authorship is an important element, both for legal reasons (e.g., you may be required to attribute the work to the author in order to avoid copyright infringement), and because it's often useful to relate multiple pieces of content by the same person, such as on a bio page with an author archive.

- **Date stamp:** News stories, blog posts, event listings, and other types of time-sensitive content usually feature a date stamp, which can mark either when the content was published or when the content is relevant, like in an event listing.

- **Subhead:** Subheads can be found intermittently throughout a piece of content, demarcating sections of information, or at the beginning of the piece, adding context and detail to a headline.

- **Summary:** These provide quick overviews of what's included in a piece of content, such as an abstract for a research paper or a boxed nut graph in a news story.

- **Bulleted or numbered lists:** Lists are tricky little beasts: sometimes, they're part and parcel with a larger, more distinct content element. But other times, they're working their own magic on a piece of content, serving up discrete information, such as specs or product features. If that's the case, be sure to label them based on what they are—e.g., specs—not just the format they're in.

- **Body content:** Beware this content element, as it's typically where large swaths of text get left to wallow shapelessly. To help prevent this, some organizations break long copy into multiple body sections, each one holding a key theme or narrative. However, many content types will have main content areas where more specific content elements aren't really discernible. If that's the case, don't try to break these into arbitrary pieces—just let it be a longer chunk.

- **Complementary content:** Often treated as a sidebar—like a timeline that accompanies a trend piece in a magazine, or a quick facts inset that provides a short overview of a story—this content is independent from the main narrative (as in, the main narrative can be read and understood without it). Like lists, when breaking them out, make sure to consider not just where the content lives on a given page, but what that content actually means—and name the content element accordingly.

- **Images and videos:** While images and videos can certainly be content types unto themselves—you've *seen* YouTube, right?—they're often simply elements of a larger piece of content, telling one part of a story or supporting other elements. It's important to decide whether a video can stand alone or is part of a more complex type of content.

- **Captions:** Working in tandem with photos, charts, graphics, or videos, captions add written context to visual content.

- **Transcripts:** Transcripts to audio content provide users with a text version, which can be useful for accessibility, SEO, and other factors. While a transcript could live on its own, divorced from its A/V companion, it is often part of a larger multimedia content type.

- **Pull quotes:** Typically larger, more graphic treatments of a quote pulled from within a story or a key message from within marketing content, pull quotes turn important or compelling information into a visual hook for readers.

- **Tags and categories:** Sometimes this information is only used for internal metadata (e.g., to help your CMS connect information or enable your CMS authors to find content), but it may be used as external-facing content as well. Tags and categories can provide access to other similar content, help set the scene for users, and increase SEO performance.

These aren't necessarily the only elements you'll need to consider. In fact, each new content type you analyze is an opportunity to identify new ones, so an exhaustive list would be, well, *exhausting*...if not impossible.

Most important, this list is generic—a starting point that will help you begin identifying the natural divisions in your content. From here, you also want to define what these elements are doing in the context of your content—for example, in a recipe, you'd have elements like "preparation time" and "ingredients." You might have elements like a "testimonial" or a "review." The more the content's meaning is reflected in the name of the element, the better.

Finally, as you work through your own content, just remember to look for elements that are both distinct from other parts and that communicate a specific piece of information.

## Structure Follows Substance

Once you're comfortable identifying content elements, your eye will start identifying them everywhere. But don't get overwhelmed; not all of these elements are of equal importance—and that's the point. You want to know everything about this content so you can determine what really matters to your users and organizations, because that's how you'll know which pieces you want to document more closely and design structures around.

Take our tale of two recipe models. While Epicurious values related recipes and meal planning guides—great ways to engage a user in more page views—my grocery client cares more about outlining the recipe's ingredients and departments where they're found as a means of getting people into the store to shop. And that's only two of the potential approaches to meaningful models, as illustrated in Figure 3.6.

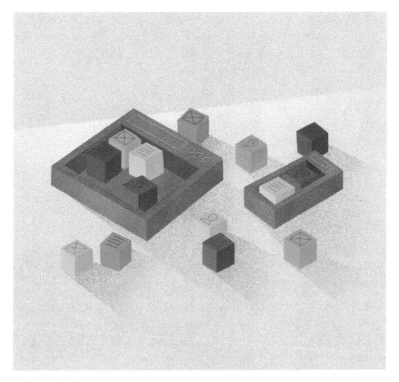

FIGURE 3.6
The same type of content might need more or fewer distinct elements, depending on what it's intended to do for your organization and your users. The right answer comes only once you've analyzed all your little pieces of content through the lens of a big-picture strategy.

That same recipe could be used in many more types of organizations and serve an entirely different purpose. For example, let's say a local artisanal cheese producer publishes its own goat cheese pizza recipe. What's this little creamery trying to accomplish? It may want to add credibility and depth to its brand story, and it probably wants to give fans ideas for what to make with its cheese so they'll—you guessed it—buy more. Meanwhile, your favorite public television cooking program could share this recipe on its site while promoting its current fundraising drive, featuring a very special pizza paddle as its thank-you gift.

In every case, the recipe could be the same, but what each element is intended to do for the organization would be entirely different—and so, the decisions you make about how those content elements will be handled must be different as well.

That's why it's not enough to simply understand the elements that make up a piece of content; you must understand how each of those elements is contributing to the piece's overall meaning—which we'll discuss in Chapter 4, as we turn this close content analysis into a documented content model.

## Coming Up for Air

OK, we've come pretty far, from business strategy to website strategy to content strategy to somewhere in much deeper waters. Time to catch our breath for a moment, get out of the weeds, and remember why we're here: because we want content that can go mobile, portable, cross-channel—everywhere. Because we want content that's smarter and more prepared for our users than ever. And because none of those things will be possible unless we truly know what our content holds.

By getting close to your content, asking hard questions, and synthesizing the answers you find, you're now armed for action. This doesn't mean every single element you've identified and dissected will get special treatment in your CMS, or get a laundry list of rules attached to it. But it does mean you will:

- Understand which elements are most critical, allowing you to prioritize how you design systems to deal with those elements without throwing things like CMS scope out the window.

- Have specific, tangible examples to guide CMS recommendations—and the analysis to back them up.

- Be able to provide content creators with a clear understanding, not just of how to "chunk" content, but why.

- Have the knowledge to collaborate with designers about layout considerations for responsive sites and mobile applications.

- Know what's important when you start talking with technical teams about things like metadata, markup, and APIs.

- Be more prepared for cross-channel or mobile projects, even if your organization isn't quite ready for them today.

Ultimately, this deep dive is all about arming you with the knowledge to act purposefully and convincing others to do the same. Without this, no number of CMS bells and whistles or markup acronyms will prepare your content for being set free.

Now we're ready for what's next: documenting our findings as complete content models, aligning them with our CMSs, and sharing it all with both the technical teams responsible for making them a reality and the authors who'll have to use them.

Onward, yes?

CHAPTER 4

# Creating
# Content Models

Documenting a Content Model                    52
Considerations and Compromises                 56
CMS Capabilities and Trade-offs                61
Authors and Workflows                          63
Turning Models into Ecosystems                 73

You may already be making content models—even if you don't know it.
That's how it happened to me.

A few years back, not long after I'd convinced my company that there was something to this "content strategy thing," I found myself inching closer and closer to the people building CMS templates, and asking more and more questions as I did. Why don't we split this blob into multiple chunks? Why can't we limit this field to 200 characters? Why isn't there a place for author attribution?

Pretty soon, I stopped asking why and started making simple bulleted lists of attributes I wanted included. I'd take these lists to the team and ask them to be included in our IA and spec documents.

I didn't have a name for this back then. Mostly, I referred to it as "making the CMS suck less," (or, sometimes, "irritating the hell out of my team"). But these bulleted lists were my very first content models. Today my documentation may be slightly more complex (though not much)—and, I hope, my models a bit better—but the approach is basically the same. Take the knowledge you gleaned from knowing your content—and its purpose—inside and out, then:

- Write down all the content types you have and all the elements each one *could* contain, based on your analysis from Chapter 3, "Breaking Content Down."

- Decide how granular to get—in other words, which of those elements you actually *need* to include.

- Discuss it with both those who will technically implement it and those who will rely on it.

- Rinse and repeat until you make it real.

Since you should now have a good draft of your content types and their potential attributes mapped out, we'll use this chapter to focus on the rest. First, we'll talk about how you can document your content model. Then we'll walk through the considerations, compromises, and collaboration opportunities you might experience as you work to get it implemented.

## Documenting a Content Model

Type "content modeling" into your favorite search engine, and you may never want to think about modeling content again. Replete with references to XML and RDF and a whole mess of acronyms, information about content modeling tends to include software-specific white papers, jargon-heavy explanations, and engineer-speak galore.

All this makes content modeling seem difficult and often too dry and distant for writers, designers, and strategists. But a content model needn't be complicated, nor even particularly technical. It just needs to be useful and clearly defined.

After all, in Chapter 3 we got at the art of the content model—the beating heart that lends it life—and looked at how two different models might be constructed for a common content type, a recipe. Sometimes, that level of modeling is enough. Other times, you might need to get more high-level, more nitty-gritty, or both to communicate your model adequately to others.

At the high level, you could create a model that shows a number of content types and how they're related to one another. For example, let's say you're working with content that doesn't just include recipes, but also additional content about the dishes those recipes make, meal plans according to cuisine types and events or holidays they're part of, ingredient descriptions, and the like. In this case, you'd show how all those types of content are conceptually connected to one another, as shown in Figure 4.1.

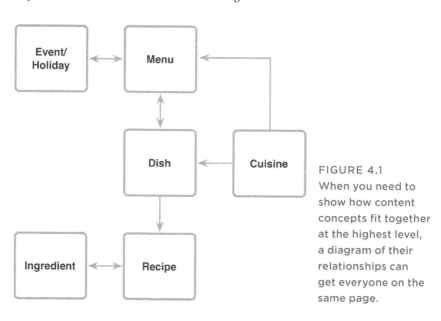

FIGURE 4.1
When you need to show how content concepts fit together at the highest level, a diagram of their relationships can get everyone on the same page.

In this chart, arrows show the relationships between types of content. Lines without an arrow indicate a singular relationship, while those with an arrow indicate multiple potential relationships. (For example, each recipe can only be for a single dish, but you can have multiple recipe options for each dish.) Typically, these relationships are called one-to-one, one-to-many, or many-to-many.

While visuals are helpful for explaining content models at the conceptual level, they aren't always great for specifics. At some point, you'll likely need a place to list your actual content elements, and also to document how much content—and which kinds—your model needs to support. This can be done in something as simple as a bulleted list of elements and their requirements for smaller projects, or a detailed spreadsheet with a tab for types of content, as shown in Figure 4.2.

| Sample Content Model: Interview Feature | | | | | |
|---|---|---|---|---|---|
| Element | Description | Example (If needed) | Max Length | Format | Required |
| Title | Headline for the interview. Appears at the top of the article and in search results or listings. | "Finally Satisfied": Mick Jagger talks music, love, and life at 69 | 80 chars | Text field | Y |
| Short Title | Short version of headline. May be used in contexts where the full headline doesn't fit. Will not appear atop the full article or with the long headline. | Mick Jagger: "Finally Satisfied" | 40 chars | Text field | Y |
| Copy Deck | Short teaser content that can be used either apart from the whole story to garner interest or as a typographically stronger lead-in to the article. | After five decades as a rock 'n' roll legend, the ever-youthful Mick Jagger opens up about his wives, lovers, children, and legacy. | 200 chars | Text field | Y |
| Intro | 2-3 paragraphs setting the stage for the interview. May be shown atop the Q&A or layered on small screens, with the Q&A appearing only when tapped. | | None | Text field | Y |
| Q&A | This is the meat of the article and can be as lengthy as needed. It will never be displayed on page without its headline, byline, and pub date. | | None | Text field | Y |
| Pull Quote | Excerpt of the interview to be used as a bold visual element within or adjacent to the story. | "People have this obsession. They want you to be like you were in 1969. They want you to, because otherwise their youth goes with you. It's very selfish, but it's understandable." | 250 chars | Text field | N |
| Main Image | Editorial image of the interview subject. | | N/A | Image | Y |
| Image Slideshow | Additional images related to the subject. | | N/A | Images | N |
| Byline | Author's name. Pulls from defined author menu; connects interviews to author bios, other content by that author. | | N/A | Menu - single select | Y |
| Pub Date | Date the article goes live. Used for chronological sorting. | | N/A | Defaults to today at creation; can override | Y |
| Category | Topical areas of the magazine. Used to determine which sections the article is found in, which subscribers it's emailed to, related items, etc. | Music, Celebrities | N/A | Menu - multi select | Y |

FIGURE 4.2

A detailed spreadsheet describing the components and relationships within each content type—in this case, an "interview"—can supplement a simpler visual model.

Whether you choose a spreadsheet, a list, a wiki, or something else entirely, at some point, you'll want something that gets specific about a number of things:

- **Required/optional rules:** For example, a headline may always be required, but a subhead may be optional.

- **Length requirements:** For example, you may want to limit story summaries to no more than 300 characters so they can display in full easily, or require that all phone numbers have at least 10 digits to ensure data quality.

- **Valid character types:** For example, you may want to dictate that only numerals may be entered in ZIP code fields.

While this detail may seem minute, these decisions are critical for content people to consider for three reasons. First, the rules you determine now are what will end up in the project's specifications—and if you've already evaluated your content and your users' needs closely, you'll be most likely to understand what's truly needed.

Second, the more care you take now, the better the resulting templates will guide those adding and updating content in the CMS in the long term—resulting in more consistent, less error-prone content entry.

Finally, whether you're the one responsible for UX documents like wireframes or you're sharing your insights with the person who is, your content model and associated rules will give crucial guidance not just for *which* elements should be present, but *how much* space each one will need.

## A Moment for Metadata

So far, we've talked a lot about the actual user-facing chunks of content in your model. But there may be a whole other universe of elements that aren't visible to those on the outside: metadata. Frequently defined as "data about data," metadata can be mega-confusing at first—mostly because it's a term people use in a whole range of ways.

I typically use "metadata" to refer to descriptive information. For example, this is a book about content strategy, information architecture, and mobile; those topics describe the contents of the book.

Metadata can also be used to mean structural components. In other words, if you define a content chunk as a "summary," that can be considered a type of metadata as well. The reason I typically don't refer to this as metadata is that it's not describing the contents of the summary—what the summary is *about*—but rather its container. Makes things less confusing, in my opinion.

What's most critical here is to remember that you'll typically need both kinds of information about your content: labels for its chunks, and tags and taxonomies that define what the content is actually about. Some of those tags and taxonomies might be externally visible things users can search and sort by, and some might be internal, visible only to your CMS users.

**NOTE** WHAT IS TAXONOMY?

*Taxonomy* might be a common term for IAs, but if you're from a marketing or editorial background, this word can feel a bit foreign. Don't fret—it's not hard to get the basics. A taxonomy is a classification system—a means of organizing information by categorizing it according to a fixed list. A classical case of this is the Linnaean taxonomy of the animal kingdom, in which all animals can be categorized. For example, in the model shown in Figure 4.2, "category" would be a type of descriptive metadata that uses a taxonomy: You can't make up new tags whenever you want, but instead must select from a defined list—a list that should, in theory, offer an accurate category for anything you'd publish on this site.[1]

---

1  For an incredibly detailed look at designing and using taxonomy in organizations, pick up Heather Hedden's *The Accidental Taxonomist* (Medford, New Jersey: Information Today, 2010).

Whether and how much metadata needs to be present in your content model depends on what you intend to do with that content—and to do that, you'll need to take some considerations into account.

## Considerations and Compromises

Now that you have a format for your model, it's time to finalize it. But before you get too tied to your diagrams, you'll want to make sure your model is ready for the real world—a world complicated by things like money, people, and technology

To do this, you'll need to consider your content against three criteria:

- **Gains and losses:** What would you gain by making the element its own piece of content, and what might you lose if you don't? Consider both business and user goals here.

- **CMS capabilities and trade-offs:** Will the CMS you're storing this in support this level of complexity—and at what cost? If you're building or implementing a new CMS, are you early enough in the project to influence it?

- **Authors and workflows:** Can your content creators and editors—and their workflow—consistently enter and manage content in this way?

As you evaluate elements against each of these questions, you can make a final decision about whether or not to include them in your model.

Let's start by talking about each of those considerations—gains and losses, CMS capabilities, and authors and workflows—separately. Then, in the last part of this chapter, we'll talk about how to work with database developers, authors, and content managers to make those attributes a reality—both at launch and as content is authored and updated over time.

### Gains and Losses

"Modeling content is a never-ending battle between flexibility and complexity," says Deane Barker, whom we met in Chapter 3. The more complex a model is—as in, the more separate elements it contains—the more ways you are able to create logic about which content is displayed where and when, as well as how that content can be found, organized, indexed, and archived.

This flexibility comes at a price. The more complex the model, the tougher it is for technical teams to implement, and the less likely it will be that content creators and managers remember to use and maintain all the fields.

In other words, there's no right amount of detail for your content model. There's only finding the balance between what that content needs to do now, what you want it to do in the future, and how much you can afford to invest in both.

If you've never done it before, it may sound daunting, but don't worry: more than anything, this is about looking closely, asking questions, and drawing connections between information—skills you've likely honed in other inter-active work, now reapplied to a more microscopic plane. Plus, it's work that can be done iteratively, tuned and improved over time. If you don't get it per-fect the first time, it's OK to come back to it later.

So how you do know how granular you need to be? There are four main things to consider for each content element.

### Will this element be used for searching or sorting?

Take an events calendar, for example. To see what's coming up this weekend, users want to be able to sort events by date—creating an obvious need to treat the date as a separate field. The same need can be seen in many other types of data, such as in online retail, where faceted search allows users to expand or refine results based on criteria like size and style.

These obvious examples of searching and sorting are just the beginning, though. Take a look at your content and consider: would this information be easier to use if you could search or sort it?

### Will it be used to relate this content to other content?

Consider our recipe example from Chapter 3. If a recipe has an author or other attribution associated with it, like a cookbook or magazine title, do you need that attribution to be its own content element? That depends: do authors have more than one article in your repository? Do you want to track recipes by author or publication and allow people to find them that way? If so (and the answer is likely yes), that byline will need its own field that relates it to that author's listing.

### Does it need to be extracted and displayed alongside other content?

Let's say you want to feature upcoming events on a homepage or list them on a results page. What content should be shown in these listings—all event details, or just the name and date with a teaser description and location? If you want relevant parts of a piece of content to appear elsewhere from the main entry, then those parts need their own element in your content model.

*Looking to take a deep dive into content modeling? Then look no further than the work of Sioux Falls, South Dakota-based Deane Barker, who's been working with data models, content management, and related issues for more than two decades. I picked Barker's brain for a few minutes to find out what those of us who didn't grow up diagramming databases ought to know to get started.*

**You've been talking about content modeling long before mobile brought it to the forefront. How has it changed—or not—over the years?**

Back in the early days, we used custom-made relational databases, which gave you maximum flexibility because you could handcraft everything. When the industry started moving to boxed content management systems, there was a significant step back where we all tried to cope with really simplistic modeling tools. Since then, the competent CMS has progressed to the point where we're approaching what we used to get by building our own custom database.

Yet the basic problems of content modeling are much the same as they were 20 years ago: it's a process of breaking down logical concepts like "a press release" into their types and attributes, and this discipline is more or less universal. Languages and implementation methods come and go, but the basic problem—identifying the attributes within content, and how they function—is eternal.

**Some folks may not know much about this history—or how to get started. What tips would you give?**

Many of the challenges you find in content modeling are basic data modeling problems, and the relational database crowd solved those decades ago: Don't duplicate data. Tend toward small particles of content. Compose complex objects by combining simpler objects.

None of this is new, but it might be a new way of thinking for you. Pick up a starter book, like *Database Design for Mere Mortals*, and try your hand at creating a custom database for something simple. You'll learn countless lessons you can apply more generally to content modeling.

### How should you decide how granular your content model should get?

In general, your content creator is your limiting factor. What can he handle? To what extent is he going to think like your content model? I love content modeling—and nothing excites me like a super-granular model—but I often lean toward something simpler because I'm thinking about the author.

Almost every model can be more granular, but you get to a point where you're introducing more complexity than your authors will understand, and the reward isn't great enough. So I'd advise you to learn to live with a few rough edges rather than pushing your content creators too far.

### What about the CMS industry—how will it need to shift to make all this a reality?

We feigned a great interest in separating content and presentation when the Web came along, but deep down we knew that a press release was only ever going to be published as a webpage. Structured content was what we always should have had, but we let ourselves get lazy.

Today, with the proliferation of mobile clients, multichannel publishing, and personalization, we're finally getting serious about the separation of content and presentation. Your press release will still be a webpage, but it may also be an update on Facebook, a Tweet, and something people see on a mobile device. These things require your content to have a new level of purity, and that means doing more than paying lip service—it means actually building our CMSs to handle this.

*For more from Barker, check out* gadgetopia.com, *where he writes smart posts more often than you'd think is possible about content modeling, the CMS industry, and a bevy of related topics.*

*Does it need to shift, resize, or be removed
altogether for some displays?*

As content gets reused and reimagined across more and more displays and devices, this question becomes increasingly difficult and increasingly critical. In fact, the decisions you make now will define what flexibility you have in how content will morph and move across devices and channels. That is, if you ever want to do things like:

- Increase or decrease one element's prominence relative to other elements.

- Shift its location (such as from a sidebar to the main column) or change its relative size when a responsive design narrows for small screens.

- Exclude it from third parties that are accessing your content through an API (which we'll dive into in Chapter 7, "Making Sense of Content APIs"), so they can access some of your content, but not all.

- Display a shorter or less complex version of the content for certain circumstances.

- Deliver different versions of the content to different customers.

- Ensure the content's headers, sections, asides, and other parts stay distinct when displayed on outputs with different displays, from smartphones to read-later apps.

- Remove it from certain devices or displays altogether.

Then you'll need those content elements to be documented in your structure. For example, if your piece of content includes a teaser or copy deck, will that content always be there, and always in the same location? What about for smartphone-sized displays? What about in an Internet-enabled car or refrigerator? If you need content to appear differently on different outputs, it likely needs to be its own chunk.

Some call this process of finalizing elements "atomizing" content, but that description can be misleading. Atoms are tiny building blocks, and creating complete structures out of them would take forever. Instead of atoms, I prefer to think about content as molecules: several atoms that work together. So when modeling content, there's no need to break content down into the tiniest pieces if it's not going to help you do anything specific. Instead, cluster them into a larger chunk so as not to overcomplicate your templates (or exasperate your content managers).

At the end of the process, you should have whittled your draft content model down to just the elements you *think* your CMS should support to meet your user and business goals. Now you just need to turn that ideal model into a realistic one by aligning it with your human and technical realities.

# CMS Capabilities and Trade-offs

Content modeling isn't just up to you; it must be implementable and technically viable in your CMS as well—and that means making a model your technical team can get behind.

What's the best way to bring your content models and requirements to those responsible for CMS selection, implementation, customization, or enhancement? Instead of making database developers feel like you're telling them how to do their job (trust me, that one *never* works), you need to collaborate. After all, they're the ones likely to let you know whether a model is too complex for your CMS, or whether you can afford to create new templates for all the content types you've documented. If you approach them right, they'll probably even be happy you're taking an interest and relieved that they won't be left guessing at what structure the content needs.

Before you go barreling down the hall to make demands, take a moment to understand where this crowd is coming from. Your content model shows how information will be entered into the CMS and displayed to users on the other end, while your developers' idea of a model likely comes from training in relational database modeling. This means that rather than thinking about how a user will experience the content or even how an editor will enter it, they are often thinking about structures with rigid definitions and roles.

Thankfully, you don't need to become a database expert to start collaborating with those who are. Instead, we can simply establish some shared vocabulary to help keep the conversation on track. The following is by no means a definitive guide, but it is a starting point—a way to begin to map the content you're working with back to concepts a database developer is likely comfortable with.

That said, typical terminology used to define elements of a data model, like our illustration in Figure 4.3, includes:

- **Entities:** Units of data that can be classified into types. In short, each content type you have is an entity—a thing about which data can be stored.

- **Relationships:** These show how different entities relate to one another, such as a restaurant listing (an entity) that is located at an address (another entity). The relationship between entities in this scenario is "located at." This is an example of a one-to-one relationship (a restaurant only has one address, and its address only has one restaurant), but they can also be one-to-many or many-to-many, as mentioned earlier in this chapter.

- **Attributes:** Essentially, the same as those content elements we've covered at length—all the chunks that make the content whole.

- **Identifiers:** Your entities' unique IDs. These are how your entities are recorded and tracked in the database, rather than the more human-friendly name of your content type.

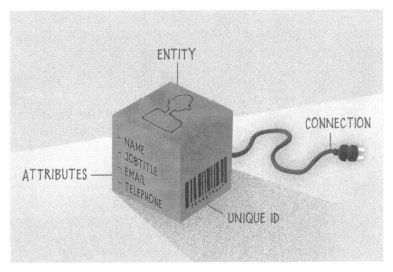

FIGURE 4.3
Data models show entities, attributes, identifiers, and how they connect to other data—or, in other words, content and how the pieces of that content come together.

In addition to thinking in these more rigid, defined terms about data, your technical team may also be thinking quite literally about *what they'll have to build* to make the model a reality. For example, a Drupal developer might hear your description of a model and say, "No, we can't do that. That goes against the way Drupal nodes work." That may well be true. But what's critical to your content isn't how the back end works; it's whether the desired effect can be achieved for both your CMS users and your audience. In other words, make sure your developers know you're less interested in following the letter of your content model than respecting its spirit.

It's also useful to walk your database developers through your model and talk about *why* you want your content to include the elements it does, so they understand what you're trying to accomplish with each. When they understand the thinking behind your decisions, they'll not only become stronger allies for your work, but will probably also suggest tweaks that make it easier to implement or are more in line with your CMS's capabilities—without losing your desired results.

# Authors and Workflows

A model is an ideal—a perfect example of what you're attempting to create. In reality, future-friendly content requires not just databases and fields, but also humans: people who will consistently adhere to the model when adding and managing content.

Humans aren't robots. They can be erratic, inconsistent, and emotional about their beloved content or defensive about their job descriptions. Which means a model doesn't have a chance of surviving unless those humans—be they writers, editors, marketing managers, communications specialists, or multiple other folks tasked with content updates and additions—understand what the content model is trying to accomplish, and how it will make their content better.

Yet, too often, those folks have no idea what the database developers intended, how certain fields work, or why it matters. To improve both the relationship and the process, your job is to serve as the bridge: the person who can understand the needs and viewpoints of both sides and make a case for all parties to adopt some new practices in the name of better, more flexible content.

Making models that are visual, and that clearly show the interconnectedness and interdependencies of your content, is the first step. But to truly help your content authors succeed, you'll also need to know a bit about the existing publishing process and how it's working for them.

If you're already involved in regular content creation and editing, you may be all too familiar with your current workflow (or lack of flow, as it may be). But for those often outside the day-to-day—like content strategists, information architects, UX designers, or any outside consultant—this analysis is a critical first step to addressing pain points and improving the author experience.

As you're evaluating the existing process and considering how it could be improved, you should keep several things in mind:

- **History:** When was the CMS implemented and why? What were the goals, and who was involved in the process? Knowing the history can help you understand underlying reasons for why things are how they are now.

- **Reviews and approvals:** Who has to approve content before it goes live? How long does it take to get content from draft to publication? How much of the workflow happens inside the CMS, and how much outside of it?

- **Complexity:** What does it take to publish content now? What will it take if your content models are implemented? Must users go through multiple screens to do it? Can they see what the end result will look like? How much does maintenance cost the organization? Understanding how complicated the system is now can help you streamline it without sacrificing structure.

- **Completeness:** Are CMS users filling out templates fully or leaving fields blank? If so, why? Are they confused, rushed, or simply unconvinced of the value of those fields? If templates are routinely incomplete, systems and logic will break down. Best to find out why—and how much it's costing your organization or affecting your users—now.

- **Consistency:** Are CMS users entering content without regard for consistency? Do multiple authors do things differently? Are they using WYSIWYG editors to override style settings, such as changing font colors and sizes? These issues point to a lack of training, but might also be due to an existing model that doesn't have what they need—so people just make it up as they go. If you can understand why they're doing it, you can determine whether you need to address the tool, the people using it, or both.

- **Training programs:** Who teaches people to use the CMS—technical teams or content-focused professionals? Do training materials talk about the content itself or just the tool? Are they written in jargon or plain language? Do they speak to how publishing content according to the guidelines supports communication and content goals? If training materials focus on features rather than processes and results, they're likely a problem.

You may always have less-than-perfect tools and people who are less than perfect at using them. But if you can be the bridge between technical teams and content managers—explain to both how the other operates, and help both get what they need—you can go a long way toward easing the CMS pain. You'll also be able to determine if the content model you're recommending is unrealistically complex for your team's workload, skill set, and priorities—and either make the case for getting them more training and resources, simplify your model, or take a staged approach.

After all, ideals are great. But the best content model is the one that actually gets used.

## Content Modeling at Work

A model may be an ideal, but we can't afford to be only idealistic. Things get messy online. Unless you're working on a brand-new presence for a brand-new company, odds are slim you're modeling content from scratch. Instead, nearly all of us must, to some extent, work with what we have: legacy content, legacy systems, and legacy workflows.

If you are implementing—or even better, considering options for—a new content management system, you're in luck. Now's the right time to make the case for clearly modeled content. But if, like many of us, you're improving your content's future one little step at a time, take heart. You can still make improvements to how content is entered and stored. You just may not be able to tackle all your content types at once.

I had that experience with the Arizona Office of Tourism, which I mentioned in Chapter 1, "Framing the New Content Challenge." While some content had been modeled when the new CMS—a customized, homegrown solution—was launched, much of the content was not (or didn't have enough structure to make it useful).

While tackling every piece of content in AOT's massive ecosystem wasn't feasible at once, we were able to quickly implement a new content model for an expensive-to-produce, yet formerly underutilized, content type: their collection of feature articles.

**TIP** WHAT SHOULD YOU FIX FIRST?

If you can't afford to restructure all your content, all at once, don't worry: content strategy is here to help. Like we talked about in Chapter 3, content strategy defines the role content should play for your organization and your users. Once you've defined your content goals and figured out the resources you have to work with, it's a lot easier to look at all your unstructured content types and decide which ones will make the most impact—and be the most feasible for your team to implement—and tackle those first.

Each month, AOT publishes a couple of these long-form features, which are written by serious writers—the kind of thing you might see in *Sunset* or *Food & Wine*. Detailing adventures across Arizona, like a tour of Frank Lloyd Wright homes in Scottsdale and Phoenix or a road trip through the Americana of old Route 66, the articles are designed to engage Arizona enthusiasts and add color and inspiration to the more practical content about attractions and accommodations.

Published monthly and promoted in AOT's email newsletter, which reaches around 150,000 subscribers, these feature articles take substantial editorial effort to produce: a trade publisher develops a content calendar, hires the writers, works with them on story development and editing, fact-checks and copyedits each piece, and delivers the final versions to AOT.

*As the chief technical officer of London-based Cognifide, a marketing technology firm that focuses on large-scale CMS projects, Cleve Gibbon knows all about the challenges of working with content, authors, and the technology that sits between them. Here are just a few of his thoughts on how to build a more future-ready publishing process.*

### What is content architecture, and where does it fit into digital projects?

Over the last 10 years, both the size and scope of Web projects increased to engage effectively with digital consumers. That created a staggering demand for real-time data and content that I call A-class: automated, accurate, aggregated, accessible, auditable, and always available. However, the large majority of business content isn't A-class; it's unstructured and inaccessible.

Content architecture is a valuable and often overlooked project phase where you structure content to add meaning and make it A-class. It's essentially adding a design phase to content management, and it makes organizations treat structured content like a business choice that needs to be invested in and designed for.

### You're known for popularizing the term "author experience." How does that fit in?

The primary users of content management systems are their authors, yet this fact is routinely forgotten—as you can see in any of the many dreadful CMS user experiences out there. We are used to working with beautiful interfaces like those provided by Google, Mailchimp, and Wufoo. They're what we all know and love. They're entry level. So why should our authors be expected to work with substandard tools to create content?

Author experience focuses upon these challenges. How can we enable authors? What can we do to make them more productive? How can we tailor the environment to make everything low effort? How can we delight authors? Because if a bad author experience leads to an even worse customer experience, we should do something to improve that.

We need to revisit old assumptions. We are no longer designing around pages, and therefore we need smarter ways for content entry—ways that are low effort and elegant, not clumsy like so many WYSIWYG text editors. We need role-based authoring, where the author's environment adapts to his specific content needs and rewards him for investing his time and effort in creating great content. Only then will an author embrace his CMS and become a loyal advocate—thus making him more productive and his content more valuable.

### What's the best way for content specialists and technical teams to work together on this?

A content model goes through various levels of detail as it moves from conceptual, to design, and into implementation. The conceptual content model is a high-level, box-and-lines drawing that aligns stakeholders around a common vision. Developers and content people then collaborate to design content architecture, which elaborates on content types and their properties, metadata, and interrelationships. The resultant content model is CMS-agnostic, but detailed enough to convey the structure and intent of content, and becomes the primary communication tool for the multidiscipline team. The build-out of the "implementation" content model falls under the purview of CMS developers, who are responsible for mapping the design content model onto something implementable and storable.

### How is the shift toward mobile and multichannel content changing your work?

Mobile is pushing structured content right onto the executive agenda. Responsive design is making our clients think long and hard about multichannel publishing. Content APIs are shining a light on how costly and uncompetitive it is to capture and store unstructured content. This is all great news because it lends credence to the business value of content architecture.

Because of this, we're getting involved in content management projects earlier, challenging existing assumptions, continually educating through example, and most importantly, listening and learning where they need help. We have to invest in taking a couple of steps backwards to design for structured content before we can help clients effectively plan, manage, and govern their content. CMS projects impact organizations massively, and it's been a real eye-opener over the last two or three years just how much. You need to be in a position to manage that change, or you'll be swept away by it.

*Cleve speaks regularly on content architecture, author experience, and all things CMS, and writes about the same at* clevegibbon.com.

With so much going into these stories, AOT wanted to get more out of them—much more than a one-time email blast. But because all those articles had originally been created as basic pages in the CMS, AOT's digital marketing manager had to paste the new articles into a new page each month and WYSIWYG them into the format she wanted: bolding the author's byline, manually linking city names to pages for those cities, and bulleting out businesses featured in the article at the end. The result (shown in Figure 4.4) was time-consuming, but it worked fine—if you never left that page.

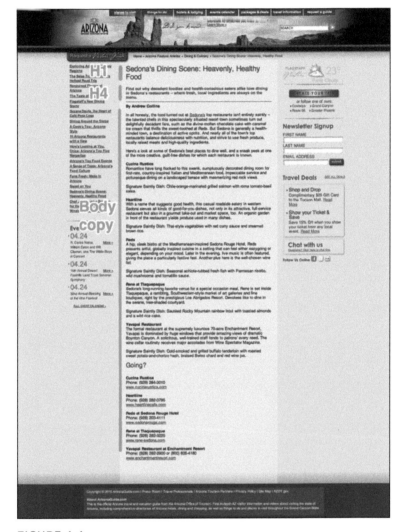

FIGURE 4.4
An example of the original feature articles, stored in unstructured, WYSIWYG-formatted pages.

But that's where the content stopped.

Relating these features to other site content—like making articles about a city accessible from that city's page—was challenging, manual, and rarely done. Those entering content didn't know why they needed to tag items, and the process was finicky and prone to error. The result was that you could be reading up on Williams, Arizona—a charming town along old Route 66—and have no idea that someone had written a carefully crafted, richly detailed account of a road trip through this very place. And if you happened to like one writer's work, forget about getting an archive of all his contributions to the site.

The problem was twofold. The content may have been engaging newsletter subscribers, but it wasn't connecting them with other information and driving them deeper. Worse, these articles were *only* reaching subscribers who had already demonstrated a commitment to the state—not the site's top (and much larger) audience: people just considering a trip to Arizona.

Moreover, AOT had bigger plans for this content. They had started sharing fresh articles on Facebook and running sidebars of older "related stories" in their newsletter, and those efforts required even more time to organize and manually publish.

To wrangle this content type into a shape fit for AOT's future, I took on the task of breaking these articles down to their elements. At first glance, they appeared minimal: a title, an author, and a big block of text, with images inserted in-line in the WYSIWYG. But looking more closely at what the articles communicated, as we talked about in Chapter 3, I found each one really needed several more elements:

- **Headline,** which set the stage for the story, caught readers' attention, and was critical to its overall meaning.

- **Copy deck,** which was a short intro blurb that played off the headline and provided an entry point to the story, employing engaging overviews and calls to action to drive readers onward.

- **Author bylines,** which lent credibility to the stories and demonstrated that they were more than marketing materials. This also, quite critically, served the state agency's requirement of not favoring one business over another by using respected third-party journalists to make editorial statements. To allow users to easily find authors' bios and see other stories by the same author, this element pulled from a separate database of author entries.

- **Images,** which provided visuals of distinctive landscapes, cultural attractions, and other only-in-Arizona elements—important for engaging prospective visitors from faraway places with the beauty of the American Southwest and adding depth to these detailed accounts.

- **Cities,** which provided geographic context for readers unfamiliar with all of Arizona's attractions and served as a point of reference for trip planners. By relating the places featured in each story to their respective cities—which already had their own content type—we could make an at-a-glance list of city links, rather than manual text links.

- **Businesses,** like hotels and restaurants. These provided entry points into tangible places to go in Arizona, allowing prospective visitors to take steps toward booking their trips and contributing to the state's tourism economy. Like cities, businesses already existed in their own database—and by tying them to articles within the content model, writers stopped adding their own listing information to the ends of articles, where it was unlikely to be maintained.

- **Themes,** like dining, the arts, or outdoors, which provided readers with a sense of the topic, and also correlated to the taxonomy already used in other content areas on the site.

Because visitors don't come to arizonaguide.com specifically to read articles, it wasn't enough for these features to live in a repository waiting for readers; they needed to come to users as they explored the more practical parts of the site, adding depth and texture to content about cities, regions, parks, and events.

Knowing this, I designed a content model using the elements outlined previously to migrate those articles out of a generic page and into a specific CMS template, as shown in Figure 4.5. From there, they can now be tagged to relevant cities, business listings, and categories of "things to do"—a taxonomical system used sitewide.

Today, the site uses these articles' content elements to build business rules, which we'll discuss in Chapter 5, "Designing Content Systems," that dictate how and when they should appear as related content throughout the site. And the articles themselves (shown in Figure 4.6) are easier to skim, understand, and use as an entry point to other content—like local cities, landmarks, and businesses that all benefit from tourist interest.

But this content isn't yet as useful as I'd like. State budgets being stagnant at best, arizonaguide.com is, as of this writing, primarily a desktop-oriented site. Its mobile site is limited to just a few features, and was built for free by a vendor that sells sponsored listings and other advertising.

Compromises and trade-offs like these are inevitable. Every organization has limitations, be they budget, resources, legislation, digital savvy, or just plain old fear. That's OK. Today, AOT's content is smarter than it was before—and when the time and budget for a flexible, device-agnostic site are available, all those feature articles and other types of content will be ready for the party.

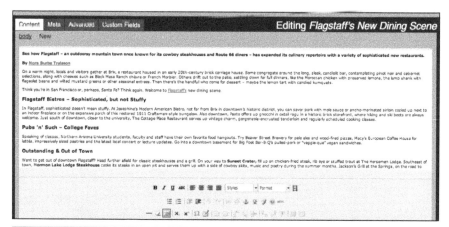

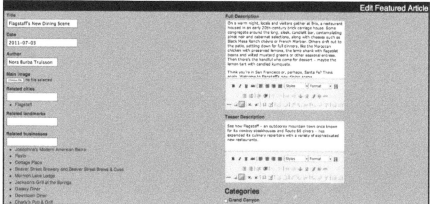

## FIGURE 4.5

The articles' CMS template, before and after. Note how that vast, wide-open text box from the old design is now broken into multiple parts.

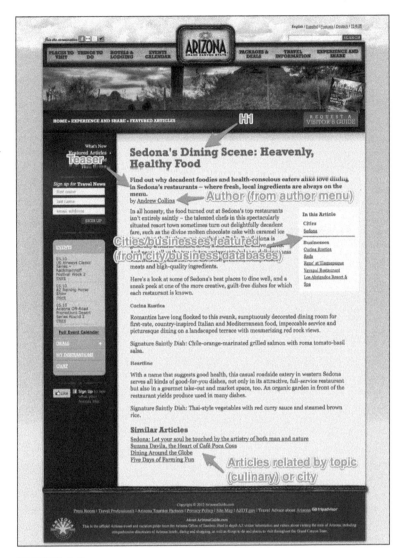

FIGURE 4.6
Detailed, informative, and written by expert travel writers, these editorially driven articles complement the Arizona Office of Tourism's more practical content perfectly—now that users can find them and use them to access other important information, like city pages and business listings.

# Turning Models into Ecosystems

Content modeling is complex work, but you already have enough expertise to get started. In this chapter, we've covered the basics for evaluating the elements you need to include, aligning them with your team, and documenting them for the world. These are things you can start doing now—even just with one critical content type. After all, some structure is often better than none.

Lending shape and structure to your information are great, but the real benefit will be when you can create a content ecosystem where all your content types work together—and your content models won't truly be finished until you do. In Chapter 5, "Designing Content Systems," we'll talk about doing this by building business rules for content—rules that dictate how your content shifts, reshapes, relates, and appears (or doesn't) as it is presented across displays and devices. With this, you can move on from how your content is entered and, in Chapters 6, "Understanding Markup," and 7, "Making Sense of Content APIs," understand how it will be stored and transported wherever and whenever you need it.

# CHAPTER 5

# Designing Content Systems

What Are Rules? 77

Why Rules Matter 79

A Framework for Rule-Making 88

Metadata is the new art direction.

—Ethan Resnick[1]

Quipped over dinner and immediately Tweeted by Karen McGrane, this gem from Resnick, an NYU student and general Internet smarty-pants, sums up so much in its six little words. As you work to publish in more places more often, designing each page manually becomes less and less viable. But instead of giving up editorial and artistic control altogether, there's another way: using your content's structure and meaning—its metadata, as Resnick puts it—to build rules that dictate how, when, and where it appears.

That's not to say we can't have nice things. The craft of manual art direction is far from dead, and will still be critical in many projects. But if you want to publish a substantial amount of content with any frequency—or maintain content that changes regularly—across many channels and devices, then it seems like rules must become, well, the rule.

In other words, when it comes to large amounts of content, we're simply going to *have* to let the robots do some of the work. The best we all can do is focus our limited stock of human care and attention toward designing systems that help them do it better—not obsessing over individual pages for individual platforms.

That's what this chapter is about: building a framework for establishing the business rules and corresponding conditional statements that support your content model and will help you keep as much editorial and presentational control as possible, while saving your limited time for manual decisions about placement and prioritization to where they'll have the most impact.

To get there, we'll break down what logic and rules really are and why they're important, and then see how they can be used in different circumstances, such as when shifting layouts in responsive design—something you're likely already working with, or at least considering. These rules will also help you create better programmatically related content and content packages that cross channels and devices. We'll then use what we've learned from each of those examples to develop a framework for evaluating your own content and determining what sorts of business rules and conditions you need.

When we're done, you'll have the tools to design your own systems of logic and relationships—tools you'll use as you work with people like developers, CMS technologists, product managers, and designers to turn your content models into ecosystems that effectively support and reveal the relationships between information.

---

1   For more on the topic from Resnick, see http://rfld.me/Olf1aM.

# What Are Rules?

In the previous chapters, we've talked about breaking content down, analyzing its elements, and designing structures to support those elements. While these content chunks are much more useful than big blobs for things like searching and sorting information and designing templates—and, if you've been involved in IA, you may have already been building some of those content chunks—their usefulness goes far beyond just that. From each of those elements, you have the ability to systematically build logic and rules that will help your content thrive.

Rules, also called *conditions*, are simply the logical statements that dictate how, when, and where something will occur. If you've done much with math, you might remember writing if-then statements: If this occurs, then that should occur as well.

The rules you'll need to make your modular content work are no different. If a page is about puppies, then display content from the pet category in the sidebar. If a user has a screen smaller than 480px wide, then remove the summary module from the sidebar and slide it between the headline and the lead in the main area. If content is made available to third parties, then only let them access content elements A, B, and D—allow C for internal use only.

## Rules Create Systems

The great thing about incorporating rule-based content is that it allows you to work in systems: sets of typical circumstances and resulting content needs, rather than endless one-off decisions about placement and priority. But it's important to note that you can't create a system unless your content is systematic as well—and that means, typically, relying on modular chunks that are consistent across all your content, rather than trying to build rules off freeform metadata (e.g., tags).

What's the problem with freeform tags? Well, when you allow authors to tag content with whatever words they choose and use that as a major form of metadata, you're going to have lots of inconsistencies: tags that were used once, tags that are similar to one another but written differently, tags that are so popular they're used for everything.

Freeform tags—often visualized as a tag cloud, as shown in Figure 5.1—can be useful for classifying large amounts of information for user retrieval or even defining what your controlled vocabulary should be in the first place, but they often won't serve your needs when creating content systems that are interconnected and rule-based, like we're doing today. Because in order to build logic around a tag, that tag must be used consistently across the entire system—something this anything-goes approach is notoriously bad at.

FIGURE 5.1
A tag cloud, the visual representation of freeform tagging, shows how little structure this approach provides, because there's no consistency in usage. Tags like these tend to work independently, rather than as a system.

### Rules Are Intrinsic

Instead of relying on the metadata you get from freeform tags, a more scalable, and reliable, way to build rules is to base your logic on one or more of the actual semantic elements within your content—the meaningful chunks you already determined in Chapter 4, "Creating Content Models," such as the location of an event, a publication date, or the author's name. Alternately, you might also base your rules off a taxonomic system, such as service or product categories.

Taxonomies *can* and *do* change over time (for example, scientific discovery has made our modern Kingdom-Phylum-Class-Order animal classification system substantially different from the original 18th century version), but they don't change often—making them more reliable for building automatic systems upon than more freeform styles of tagging.

The more you can use the semantic chunks that are inherent to the content itself, or taxonomies that rarely change, rather than relying on a set of classification options that's more fluid and unreliable, the more likely they are to be consistent across all your content, and to remain relevant through changes in things like trends, campaigns, and content authors.

# Why Rules Matter

In Part III, "Putting Structured Content to Work," we'll be taking a deeper look at how structure and rules are enabling organizations to do all sorts of things, from determining how content appears in mobile devices to what happens when it's shared with third parties to how collections of content are deeply linked and interconnected. But to understand the importance of your content attributes right now, let's take a quick look at why rules matter in making content go further.

## Related and Contextual Content

Content that appears in sidebars or other related areas often falls into one of three rather limiting categories:

1. Static and hard-coded into the page or template.

2. Dynamically displayed based on one or two metadata elements, such as content type and recency (for example, "show most recent three press releases").

3. Manual, entered and maintained by hand at the page level.

In the face of both your users' needs and your business goals, all three of these options fall flat, either offering too little relevance to users, failing to drive people toward desired actions, or simply taking too much time and resources to manage and maintain.

By relying instead on the elements within a piece of content to create thematically linked, automatically updated related items, you can sustainably manage collections of content that are more useful for users and easier on your budget.

Let's look at an example. Remember the Arizona Office of Tourism from Chapter 1, "Framing the New Content Challenge"? Based on analytics data like search engine keywords, users' site search terms, and most-visited pages, I knew AOT's audience wanted to look up a city they'd be visiting and see what was around it. But the city database didn't include much content—and, on its own, produced lifeless, less-than-useful listings, like that page about Sedona we looked at.

Despite making huge improvements to consistency, style, topic breadth, and SEO during the site redesign, the content was broken at a structural level. All the time improving copy in the world couldn't fix it.

So what did my team do? We went back to our site architecture. The site's structure, while logical at a high level, disintegrated quickly into page stacks, never fully documenting the content's depths. Moreover, the system was purely hierarchical, as shown in Figure 5.2: "Places to Visit" branched into regions and cities. "Things to Do" branched into activity categories and business listings. Landmarks—like state and national parks, natural spaces, and historical sites—were in the "places" section, but stored in another database entirely.

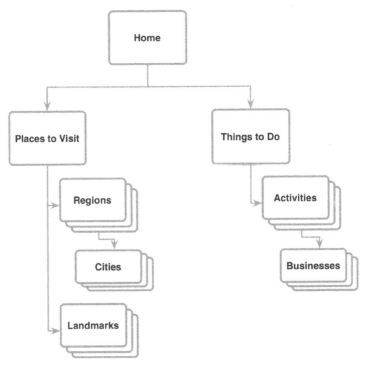

FIGURE 5.2

An excerpt of the Arizona Office of Tourism's original site structure: all hierarchy, no relationships between information.

Meanwhile, the site's editorial content, including itineraries and feature articles written by professional travel writers for the state's monthly e-newsletter, were treated as basic pages, added in big content blocks with a WYSIWYG editor whenever necessary. Without structure to these stories, there was no systematic way to tie them to the cities where they'd be most relevant, nor for a user to search and sort for similar stories that piqued her interest. So there sat a handful of rich, engaging features about Sedona's romantic restaurants, healthy spa retreats, and local vineyards—disconnected, forgotten, and not doing their job of getting users excited and helping them plan trips. In a site with tens of thousands of pages and nearly 400 cities to manage, no one was about to add (much less maintain) text links for all of them.

If AOT was going to offer governable, useful, and compelling content to meet one of its users' top tasks, then I needed to solve this disconnect. I did this by breaking down previously unstructured content like articles and itineraries and building a structure that revealed and strengthened the relationships already inherent within them, as shown in Figure 5.3. This allowed us to tie everything together with rules that were based on shared attributes— namely, the city or cities to which each piece of content was related.

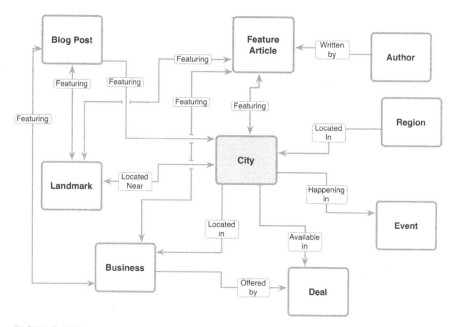

FIGURE 5.3

This high-level model showed the different types of content the system would support, as well as the content elements that would be required to connect them.

What's this mean? Take, for example, that page about Sedona shown in Figure 5.4. It, along with pages for each of Arizona's nearly 400 cities, is now bolstered by rich, related information, including listings for local, state, and national parks, city-specific travel deals and events, and, of course, those detailed feature articles and itineraries.

Across the site—and especially in these top pages—content has become more connected and relevant. And because relationships are based on rules, such as a landmark's proximity to a city, it requires little manual management of tags and links. When new businesses or articles are added, they simply appear all the places they're supposed to.

Solving problems like these may seem time-consuming, but here's the silver lining: Because you've already figured out your content types, elements, and priorities, you're intimately familiar with what you have to work with—which means you'll have a much easier time determining how to build rules based off them and even refine them based on new business needs, content performance, or user feedback.

FIGURE 5.4
The new page for Sedona, where conditions dictate the content that appears—for example, displaying landmarks like national parks and monuments whose ZIP codes are within a defined radius of Sedona's.

## Content Rules for Responsive Designs

Responsive design has been a wildly popular topic in recent years, with organizations of all sizes rushing to redesign their sites to flex for different devices. As Ethan Marcotte writes, the movement is all about "embrac[ing] the flexibility inherent to the web, without surrendering the control we require as designers."[2]

Sounds a lot like what we're trying to accomplish with content, right?

To do this, responsive design calls for building sites using flexible grid layouts, flexible images and media, and CSS3 media queries. Together, this allows the site's layout to shift on the fly based on the display size of a user's device. The result is a single website that responds to the device you're on, delivering the same content in a way that's optimized for that device's display.

While flexible grids, flexible images, and media queries may be the functional backbone of going responsive, there's more to it than that. Because as layouts shift and change, it's critical to keep your focus on what's important for your users—and to ensure the priorities and relationships between content stay intact.

On a small scale, for a site that's just a few pages or only supports one kind of content, this might be simple. And that's why some of the most striking responsive design samples have come from places like blogs and personal websites. But once you scale up to include corporations, online publications, universities, government offices, and other organizations with large swaths of content to account for, things get a bit trickier.

Take Starbucks, for example, which launched a sparkly, new, responsive website in early 2012, as shown in its three main configurations in Figure 5.5.

FIGURE 5.5
Starbucks was one of the first big brands to go responsive in early 2012. Here's their site rendered on a laptop, an iPad, and an iPhone.

But how does priority shift as screen size changes? Let's look at a couple examples.

Say a user is interested in the Clover—a super-fancy coffee machine company that Starbucks bought a few years back and now operates in select stores. She'll find a thorough page about the Clover pretty easily, as shown in Figure 5.6.

---

2   Ethan Marcotte, *Responsive Web Design*, Chapter 1 (New York: A Book Apart, 2011).

FIGURE 5.6

Starbucks' desktop-sized page about its Clover coffee machine, available only in select stores. Click the right-hand module to find out which ones.

## The Clover® Brewing System

Tweet  8+1  Like  1.2k

Only once in a while does a true innovation like this come along.

For decades, the technology of coffee brewing had been well established. But in 2007, a new technology made its debut that totally changed the game.

That development was the Clover® brewing system: an innovative design that lets you discover new layers and dimensions within a coffee's familiar aroma, flavor, body and acidity. The result is a deeper experience – one that's carefully prepared and made to order, one cup at a time. You can find Clover® brewing machines in select Starbucks stores.

The Machine

The Clover® brewing system uses innovative Vacuum-Press™ technology to create your cup right in front of you. You watch as a stainless steel filter lowers into the brew chamber. Hot water is added at a precise temperature to brew your coffee for an ideal length of time.

The Clover® brewing system controls brew time and temperature digitally, as even small changes here can dramatically affect the outcome you taste in the cup. A thermal blanket surrounds the brew chamber to keep water within 1 degree Fahrenheit of the ideal temperature.

After the coffee brews, it is pulled through a 70-micron filter. The resulting grounds are pushed out of the top of the machine. The coffee itself flows into your cup – hot, aromatic and amazingly flavorful. We're pretty sure it will be the best cup of coffee you've ever tasted.

The Beans

On the desktop, the visual priority's pretty clear: overview, where you can find a store with a Clover, and then deeper content about the machine and why it brews such a phenomenal cup of coffee. But look again at that smartphone-sized version shown in Figure 5.7, and all you'll see is the image, headline, and 400 words of marketing copy: about the machine, the process, and even a long digression about the quality of Starbucks' beans. Only then—far, far down the page—do you get a link to actually find out where you can get a cup of Clover coffee.

Why is the Clover-equipped store finder so separated from the content at the top of the page? Two reasons. First, the main content is written in one big copy blob, so there are no "chunks" where you can divide the content into parts and insert an element in the middle. The second is a lack of logical rules.

Spend some more time around Starbucks' site, and you'll find that pretty much all their templates work the same way: desktop- and tablet-sized layouts include a right-hand sidebar, and smartphone-sized displays simply plop that content onto the bottom of the page.

Sometimes, it works just fine—like when the sidebar features information unrelated to the page, such as entering Starbucks' Idea Challenge. But let's see what happens when you check out some fancy beans to brew, as shown in Figures 5.8 and 5.9.

Find the Ultimate Cup of Coffee

Does a Starbucks near you have the Clover® brewing system? Find out.

Got a Great Idea?

my STARBUCKS IDEA

We want it! Share your ideas and see what other people are suggesting at My Starbucks Idea.

Coffee  .  The Clover® Brewing System

The Clover® Brewing System

Browse by Profile          Browse by Form

**FIGURE 5.7**

The same page displayed on an iPhone. Note how much harder it is to figure out where you can buy a dang cup of Clover coffee.

FIGURE 5.8
The desktop-sized page for Starbucks Reserve Malawi Lake of Stars coffee. See how easy it is to skim the beans' stats and click to buy it?

### Starbucks Reserve®
### Malawi Lake of Stars

The third largest lake in Africa borders a nation landscaped with towering mountains and lush valleys.

It's called the Lake of Stars, after the sparkling reflections that lights from drifting boats bounce off the surface at night, and it's this magical landmark that lends our Starbucks Reserve® coffee from Malawi its name.

Malawi provides one of the smallest coffee yields in East Africa - only once before have we had the opportunity to offer a single origin coffee from this stunning landlocked country. But like the glimmering lake, this is a coffee with its own chance to shine. Full bodied and well balanced, soft florals and notes of orange spice and chocolate take center stage in this rare gem from East Africa.

Customer Reviews

Malawi Lake of Stars? Floral notes and spicy-chocolaty flavor? Don't mind if I do. But wait: Where'd my "buy now" button go on mobile? Where are the fast facts about this bean's provenance? Again, Starbucks' rule is to bump the sidebar to the bottom—and this time, it might be affecting their sales.

Starbucks' responsive site brings the company a long way toward future-friendliness. But couldn't these content decisions make the site stronger *and* keep the company's message better intact?

In other words: getting responsive isn't just a design-and-dev problem. It's a content problem.

Thankfully, it's one you're now prepared to solve. Rather than building every template off the same rule—that the sidebar flips below main content as the screen size narrows—Starbucks, and the many other organizations currently relying on this in their responsive designs, could take a more meaningful approach, making different decisions about how layout should shift for each type of content.

This is why it's so important to have meaningful structure and the right rules to match—because without it, you might turn a beautiful responsive site into a lost opportunity for your organization and a frustration point for your users.

FIGURE 5.9

But on a smartphone, once again that content gets buried—this time below a near-endless scroll through marketing copy and buyer reviews. Don't they want to sell the beans?

### Many Ways to Make a Whole

Adopting this thinking about rules, relationships, and priorities can help you do even more complex things than switch layouts or create smarter related items. It will help you build a system that's ready to deliver multiple combinations of content elements to different devices, products, or channels.

Let's see this in action with our friends at NPR. Unlike a responsive website or related items on a single site, NPR uses content models and rules to publish the same story using different combinations of its content elements across various presentation layers—such as the NPR website, NPR Music, NPR iPhone app, NPR iPad app, and affiliate station websites, as we talked about way back in Chapter 2, "Building a Way Forward."

To accomplish this, NPR had to make major decisions not just about which content elements would exist in its CMS templates, but also how those content elements would be combined and displayed for different products in a way that would offer the best content for each platform while also respecting the meaning and message of that story.

So how did NPR decide what stays and what goes, and which content elements would create the right shape for a given presentation? They did this by handing editorial control to each platform, where someone familiar with that platform's strengths and weaknesses—and its target users—could determine which content elements made sense within that experience. For example, your local member station might want to include the full-length written version of a story on their site, while those running the NPR.org Player could opt to only include the title, teaser, date, and audio.

That doesn't mean NPR's control over content is completely decentralized. Whereas a wire service, like the Associated Press, allows members to use chunks of content any way they want as long as they attribute the story properly, NPR keeps its content connected by limiting the ways that platforms can slice content apart.

But this approach was only possible when NPR stopped labeling its content chunks by their location on the page—such as "sidebar"—and started labeling them in a more semantic way, calling them names like "timeline" or "quick facts." Because only then could NPR know what each element was doing on the page and whether it was needed.

## A Framework for Rule-Making

If you're typically most comfortable considering your content in terms of Word documents and webpages, this kind of thinking—about rules and conditions, chunks and logic—will be a bit of a shift. But now that you've spent the time to break your content into parts and design meaningful models for it, it's just one more step to get comfortable with conditional statements.

Depending on your specific industry or project, you might also want to start thinking more like a product designer: for each output of your content, you're delivering a product—be that a website, a mobile app, an ebook, or even a printed piece. In this context, your decisions all align around the goal of making each product the strongest and most useful it can be, incorporating content in the way that will best support it.

In order to make rules that respect your communication goals, your products' capabilities and restraints, and, of course, the people who will be consuming your content, you need to do some thinking about what role each micro element in your content model should play in creating a whole—because only once you know what a piece of content needs to *do* can you decide where it needs to *go*.

To do this, you'll need to start considering how your content elements support your communication goals—and your users—by evaluating each of those carefully crafted chunks in three key areas: meaning, priority, and relationships. Let's look at each.

## Meaning

As we first talked about in Chapter 4, each element should be contributing something specific to the overall piece of content—or it shouldn't be there at all. To assess a specific element's meaning, begin by asking questions like:

- What does communicating this information do for the audience? For the organization?

- What meaning is lost if this element goes away? Are there users this will affect most?

- How critical is this element to making the content feel whole? Does it need to exist at all times, or could we afford to drop it in some contexts?

## Priority

When you understand the relative importance of a content element to the others it appears with, you can better gauge how it should be prioritized on any given layout. To gauge its priority, ask yourself several questions:

- How—and how much—does this element contribute to the content's purpose?

- Does this element drive sales or contribute to business goals in some way?

- Does it provide access to a key user task?

- Is this element more important for users in certain contexts, such as on an app, and less important for those in others, such as on a mobile-optimized site? Which contexts, and how do you know? Can you test this?

Be careful about assumptions here, though. It's easy to say "smartphone users are on the go, so detail isn't important to them," but are you sure that's true? As we'll discuss in depth in Chapter 8, "Findable Content," you need to be pretty confident about what's important to your users before scrapping content on small screens.

## Relationships

Content elements don't stand alone. They work with one another to form meaning and tell stories. When you assess your content's relationships, you discover which pieces need to work together, and how—or you risk breaking narratives or interrupting the buying process, as we saw Starbucks' responsive site do. You can avoid these problems by asking questions like:

- What relationships exist between this element and others? Are those relationships hierarchical, like parent and child; interdependent, like spouses; or complementary, like friends? For example, an image and its caption may be interdependent and impossible to split, while a timeline sidebar may be a child story related to its larger parent feature and easier to break off.

- Can this element appear alone and still provide value to users, or does it become meaningless? If not, what other elements must be kept with it to keep the meaning intact?

- If this element changes or disappears, what other elements are affected?

Meaning. Priority. Relationships. All right, you have the questions. But what might the answers look like?

To find out, let's return to our Epicurious example from Chapter 3, "Breaking Content Down." As we conjectured then, Epicurious is a publisher that makes money on ad revenue, which typically comes from increased impressions generated through page views. Meanwhile, users want to find something to cook that meets their dietary, meal type, or ingredient requirements. As a result, an Epicurious recipe is likely designed to be compelling, specific, and connected—so users want to make it, can easily tell whether it meets their needs, and want to visit additional Epicurious content.

Let's say that Epicurious wanted to continue meeting these macro goals on a new mobile-optimized site or responsive redesign, and you're trying to figure out the best way to make it so. How would you determine what rules to put in place? By keeping these business and user goals in mind, you could begin to make plenty of decisions about how each element of content will function. Here are just a few potential outcomes:

*Meaning*

- The image doesn't help users make the recipe, but it provides an instant point of reference for them. If you tease the recipe sans image, it might reduce users' interest in cooking, and therefore clicking, it. Therefore, it's essential to keep an image thumbnail alongside the title at all times.

- Teaser copy adds a pleasant spin to the recipe, providing users with a rich sense of what this dish is like. How much does this copy affect users' understanding of, and interest in, this recipe? If the description strikes an emotional or physical connection with the food that the recipe alone cannot, then you might make a rule that keeps it intact across platforms. This should be tested with users.

*Priority*

- Smaller screen sizes shouldn't be served recipes without related items to reduce clutter, because it will decrease Epicurious' page views and threaten the business model.

- Wine pairings and related menus are corollary to the recipe—great for specialty situations, but not critical to the recipe itself. If analytics data says readers don't use them often, then consider linking to them on smaller screens, rather than displaying them on the page. However, related recipes should stay because readers use this feature regularly.

*Relationships*

- Ratings influence whether users want to make the recipe, so this content should always connect to the recipe title and teaser. If the sidebar were to get pushed below main content for smaller screens, the rating would be much harder to find, and potentially frustrating. Instead, ratings must follow recipe titles in layouts, and never be pushed below ingredients and directions.

- When split from the teaser description, this title is very descriptive and may be able to stand alone, but is this consistent across recipes? If not, then teasers should always appear with their titles.

As you can quickly see, simply pushing a sidebar to the bottom or removing all but the most basic recipe elements is unlikely to meet anyone's needs here. Instead, there are a range of considerations and a whole host of potential outcomes for Epicurious—and likely for your own content, too.

While some of these decisions should lead to testing and user research, the content alone—when you get close enough—has more answers than you may think. And, just as important, it reveals plenty of interesting questions as well.

## Implementing the Rules

How your content's rules and conditions will be implemented will vary: Some may be built into your CMS's modules. Others might be implemented via CSS and media queries in a responsive design. And still others might be on the other side of an API—a solution more and more organizations are adopting to publish content to multiple sites, devices, and experiences that we'll talk about at length in Chapter 7, "Making Sense of Content APIs."

But with this framework, you should be prepared to begin evaluating what sorts of logic you'll need to make your content ecosystem work—and be ready to talk about markup, the bit of code that your content elements might need before they're ready to travel. In Chapter 6, "Understanding Markup," we'll talk about what markup is, how it works, and the types of markup you might encounter as you're working to make your content more flexible.

# Understanding Markup

| | |
|---|---|
| Markup Matters | 96 |
| Many Meanings, Many Markups | 96 |
| What's Your CMS Got to Do with It? | 98 |
| The Semantics of…"Semantic" | 99 |
| The Lowdown on Markdown | 104 |
| Many Ways to Get to Markup | 106 |
| The Secret to Markup | 107 |

You have an understanding of your content's inherent structure. You've thought about its descriptive metadata, and about the rules and conditions that will help give it life. But how will it keep that shape and form as it travels beyond your CMS and outside the bounds of a single site?

More often than not, the answer is markup.

Just like an editor marks up a book before it goes to print—adding in-line notes that dictate where a block quote should start and stop, or when to use bullets—markup is a way to add directions to your content about what different pieces of text are, allowing you to make automated decisions about what those pieces of text should do when they're displayed. In other words, it's the code that wraps around your content chunks and lends them machine-readable meaning.

In this chapter, we'll take a look at why markup matters for content, explore the types of markup you may hear mentioned in conversations with technical teams (as well as which ones are likely to be used by whom), and see why knowing just a bit about this oft-mystified m-word can help you make better decisions about how you plan, structure, write, and share content.

## Markup Matters

Let's say you've got some bright, shiny new content. It's brilliant! It's perfect! It's ready! Yet all that care you've given it won't matter one bit if the systems it encounters on its way to publication don't understand what it is and what to do with it. This content, smart and stylish as it might seem at first, is silent—incapable of describing itself to anyone but a human who's actually reading it.

That's how markup can help: It gives your content a voice that other machines can understand, making it capable of describing itself and allowing it to keep its style and soul intact as it flexes to meet the demands of different devices and experiences.

## Many Meanings, Many Markups

But what is markup, really? It can seem a little opaque to the uninitiated, but don't let that slow you down. It's simply code that carries the content chunks and metadata you've already outlined wherever they need to go. The code itself might vary depending on the type of markup you're using (more on that later, don't worry). But the idea is about the same: wrapped around each meaningful bit is a snippet of code that tells machines what that chunk is.

In addition to marking up the chunks of content your users actually consume, markup also lends any descriptive metadata you've collected about a piece of content a life of its own—so if that copy deck is from a story about, say, the city of San Francisco, you'd want markup that keeps that topical tag with the content as well.

At a very basic level, you can divide markup approaches into two categories: the stuff designed to make it look pretty, and the stuff that actually makes it smarter.

## Presentational

If you're used to a word processor like Microsoft Word, presentational markup is the equivalent of changing your font to bold and 18 point every time you want to make a headline, as opposed to using Word's "styles" section, where you can label those headlines as headings instead of simply making them bigger. When you mark up content with presentation tags, you'll only be able to describe how the content should look—like adding an HTML <font color="purple"> tag to turn a specific line of text a lovely shade of lilac, or increasing font size for emphasis. You usually add it directly into the content's HTML or using the WYSIWYG editor in a CMS, hit preview, and ta-da: everything looks perfect (well, if you like purple, I guess).

Or does it? Let's say you want to make a headline stand out, so you beef the font size up by 20 points and take a peek at the page on your desktop. Perfect. But then let's say that same content will eventually be seen on a mobile-optimized version of the site, on a partner's site, and on a Kindle. Does that mega-size headline fit all those different formats? Does that formatting even render on all those screens? And what happens next year, when you update your branding and have to manually go through and replace all that presentational markup with whatever the new style guide dictates?

In a sense, this kind of markup is a lot like makeup. While my olive-skinned friend looks fantastic in scarlet lipstick, that same shade gives my face a particularly ghastly pallor. We may both want to emphasize our lips, but that doesn't mean we should use the same color to do so.

When you use presentational markup, that's precisely what you're doing: locking content into just one shade, one way to look...even when it's being displayed in places where it looks silly.

If you can't be sure exactly where and how your content is going to be displayed, both now and in the future, then purely presentational markup simply doesn't have enough power to pass muster.

## Semantic

Semantic markup, on the other hand, is designed to reveal, in a machine-readable way, the intrinsic meaning in your content, and to provide the machines that read it information they can use to apply a style sheet that determines how it should be displayed. It gives your content information about itself—telling it things like "this is a headline," rather than "this should be in large type."

The further away from a traditional "desktop website" your content travels, the more this distinction matters—because those entering content will never be able to anticipate, much less design their content around, all the different (and unknown) places and devices where it might be viewed.

Semantic markup is useful because it allows those putting content into the system to control their work's *meaning*, while leaving control for how it *looks* to those responsible for the platform where that content will be seen. That is, instead of dictating design from inside the database, aesthetics are controlled at the output level.

Remember the concept of "metadata is the new art direction" from Chapter 5, "Designing Content Systems"? Well, the more self-aware your content is, the easier it is to implement those rule-based layouts—and, you know, make them not suck. And the more you, the one who's taken time to know your content well, are involved in this work, the better that markup will be.

In short, semantic markup is the code that keeps all that thinking you did in Chapters 3, 4, and 5 intact—the code that ensures your carefully modeled content, and the meaning that structure gives it, stay strong, allowing it to withstand the stresses of shifting across time and space. And it's precisely this sort of markup—the markup that says to "emphasize the lips," rather than "use red lipstick"—that we want to focus our discussion on today.

## What's Your CMS Got to Do with It?

If you're used to authoring content in a CMS, all this talk of code wrapping around your content might seem out of place. Isn't that what the CMS is for? Well, yes...sort of. But here's the deal: When you enter content in a CMS, you're dealing with its interfaces—the external-facing screens that allow you to manipulate the content that's stored in an underlying database.

When your CMS interfaces match up with your content model, showing fields for each of the critical components rather than a wide-open text box with a WYSIWYG editor, then the content you're sending into that underlying database will be structured. From there, markup that matches your content model can be applied automatically.

Many CMSs aren't quite there yet, and so authors and editors add presentational markup to their text for good reasons: because it seems to give them some control over how it looks. The problem is, when this happens, that presentational information—like our lilac example—gets stored right alongside the content itself, forever. And the result makes for content that's messy and less manageable over time.

Instead, the future demands that content be stored in a way that's independent of the code that marks it up, but structured so it can be translated to use whatever markup you need—and, as you'll see in a moment, there are many types of markup out there.

While not all CMSs are prepared for this sort of content management today, the only way they're going to get better is if folks like you and I start asking them to.

# The Semantics of..."Semantic"

All right, you understand that markup exists, and that it helps your content retain the meaning and relationships you've already defined. Now let's get into the confusing bit. Because unfortunately, the term "semantic markup" is, well, semantically a little unclear. As you start working with structured content, you're likely to hear many people talk about semantic markup, yet meaning substantially different things.

Broadly speaking, these folks tend to be talking about either HTML (or HTML-like) markup formats, or much more complex, enterprise-level structural markup. Let's take a moment to learn about both, so you can get more comfortable when they come up in conversation.

## HTML Markup

Until recently, HTML included fairly limited semantic markup—that is, you could label a main headline with an <H1> or a chunk of text to be emphasized with <em>, rather than simply changing the font size or using the <i> tag for italics. While these tags are semantic—as in, they refer to the content's substance rather than its presentation—they're fairly weak, giving us little to go by when it comes to what the content actually *means*.

Today, however, the semantic possibilities of HTML have increased substantially, allowing people to use several approaches to HTML-based markup that give content much more semantic richness.

### Microformats

Microformats are an open data standard that builds on HTML to add metadata to pieces of content, identifying information as something specific, like a "person" or a "location." Because microformats are an open standard, many industries and organizations have added new microformats for specialty data. They work by adding specific classes to snippets of HTML, with those classes defining what the content within the snippet is. Microformats can be used to lend machine-readable meaning to chunks of incredibly small pieces of content, like a date or time, even if it's in the middle of a paragraph of other text.

### HTML5 Microdata

New in the HTML5 spec is the microdata extension, which is built off earlier microformats work. Microdata goes beyond traditional presentational HTML tags and allows you to mark up content with standards-compliant, semantically rich HTML—for example, marking up content as an "event" or "organization." However, HTML5 is, as of this writing, still in working draft status. That means not all of these new extensions are universally supported, and some may not reach mass adoption.

### Schema.org

Schema.org is an HTML5-based approach launched in 2010 by Bing, Google, and Yahoo! Designed to create a common language across search engines, Schema.org arranges HTML5 microdata into taxonomies of content types that start broadly and branch into ever-more-specific elements. Its provenance in the big search engines may give it some weight and staying power, but it's also contested by those who see it as two big players attempting to force their ontology onto everyone else.

Taken together, all these HTML-based markup approaches represent a way to make chunks of content much easier for machines to read and parse, and for information like dates, addresses, people, and other common entities to be universally understood. However, the meaning you can glean from any of these forms of markup is still somewhat limited. For example, while HTML5 now offers an "aside" tag to use for information that's secondary to the main content, there's nothing about that tag that would give a system receiving that content information about what that aside actually is, or how it fits into the rest of the content with which it's associated.

## Structural Markup

That's where the *other* kind of semantic markup comes in. Those in fields like technical communications tend to take a more enterprise-level approach to markup, creating massive systems of content structure that are comparable to databases. Unlike HTML markup and its limited semantic elements like "aside," this sort of markup is generally capable of as many specifics as you need.

For example, let's say you have a chunk of content you've defined in your model as a copy deck—a short teaser that leads into a story. With these types of markup, that content would be stored as a copy deck in your database, and a label would then be present in the markup for that content when it's displayed beyond the database. If that content travels to a system using a common language, the receiving system will immediately know it's a copy deck.

There are several common approaches to this kind of markup that you might hear about.

## XML

The mother of many markup approaches, XML (Extensible Markup Language) is designed to structure, store, and transport information using a set of rules to mark up text with metadata. As opposed to HTML, XML allows you to define your own tags, so you're not limited to a preset list of entities (that's why it's called "extensible"). Because of this, it forms the basis for a number of the other markup approaches listed next, but this also gives XML plenty of critics who say it's too clunky and difficult to write and use, as well as those who say it's too generic to be a standard.

## RDF

RDF, which stands for Resource Description Framework, is a generic method used to describe concepts—specifically, to describe things and their relationships with other things. It can be written using a variety of other languages, including both XML and JSON. It's the glue that holds linked data together, providing a language for describing data by using three elements to form a machine-readable statement: a subject, a predicate, and an object—such as stating that the Declaration of Independence has an author of Thomas Jefferson. However, in practice, RDF is currently used relatively little.

## OWL

Web ontology language, somewhat confusingly abbreviated as OWL, is built on RDF and expressed using XML. It has more vocabulary than RDF, and can therefore express more complex relationships and richer properties. For example, you can create a single statement to express that two concepts have a symmetrical relationship—e.g., not just that my husband is my spouse, but also that his spouse is me. With RDF alone, this would take two statements to communicate.

## DITA

If you've worked with—or as—a technical communicator, you've likely heard of the XML-based data model called DITA, or Darwin Information Type Architecture. Designed by IBM to handle its own technical content, DITA works with modularized content to organize it into categories based on topic. Because of this, it tends to be really good at structuring things like help content, but may not be useful for all kinds of content.

## JSON

If you start paying attention to markup conversations, you'll probably also hear a lot about JSON—and particularly how it compares to XML, with proponents and detractors on both sides. JSON, or JavaScript Object Notation, is a lightweight data interchange format designed to be easier to read and write, and also easier for computers to parse, than XML. Many organizations now offer both JSON and XML versions of their APIs, which we'll talk about at length in Chapter 7, "Making Sense of Content APIs," making the same structured content available in either language.

OWL, RDF, DITA, blah blah blah. All these markup languages can be hard to keep track of, especially if your job is more about the how and why of content than determining the best XML-based languages for API-driven mash-ups or whatever. Rather than getting lost in all the acronyms, it's probably best to just understand that these different approaches exist, have a basic understanding of what they mean, and be ready to delve into specifics about their implication for your content's structure later, when or if the need arises.

Ultimately, just keep in mind that your content will eventually become code. The more you know about how these systems work and what's being used for what, the better you can evaluate your content's needs against them and the more you can participate in conversations with those on the database end of the spectrum.

## What About the Semantic Web?

Once you understand a bit about markup, and about making content machine-readable and interoperable, then it's time to consider some of the exciting stuff that markup makes possible. One of those things is the Semantic Web: a Web where all content shares a common framework and can be shared, reused, and understood across systems—to the point where, say, machines know whether the term "blackberry" is referring to the fruit or the phone.

A completely semantic Web is a lofty goal—one not without its detractors, I might note—and our path toward it is still meandering at best. But a *more semantic* Web seems closer than ever with the recent advent of linked data, which is made possible through structured content and markup.

Coined by Tim Berners-Lee—yes, the guy who invented the World Wide Web—in 2006, linked data means exactly what it sounds like: bits of information that are linked to other, equivalent sets of data elsewhere on the Internet (often referred to as "in the cloud"), as illustrated in Figure 6.1. The idea is that, as opposed to HTML links, which link one document (e.g., a page) to another, linked data connects the things those pages are about by connecting the actual data behind those two pages instead. This gives both databases access to the information in the other, and that information then becomes more useful to both people and machines.

FIGURE 6.1
Linked data connects content from different places, like between
your website and Wikipedia, based on shared content attributes—
and it's getting more and more useful for connecting content
across sources.

For example, consider *The New York Times*. Since the 19th century, it's
been maintaining a tremendous index of people, organizations, places,
and descriptors in the news. Starting in 1913, it began publishing that
data first in a quarterly index, and later an annual one.[1] Now that its
collection has been digitized, the *Times* has opened it up as linked data at
http://data.nytimes.com, making this extensive list of topics—well over
10,000 as of this writing, with plans to continually add more—accessible to
anyone who wants it.

What can you do with information like this? All kinds of things. At a basic
level, you could extract links to all the stories about Syria. Getting more
complex, you could automatically pull in detailed definitions, bios, and other
supplementary content that your organization could never produce and
maintain itself, richening your users' experience without increasing your
content production needs. And you can do all this without relying on time-
consuming manual linking, or less-than-relevant automated content based
on simple tags.

---

1   See more of the story at http://rfld.me/M2dsyy.

If you're preparing content for the future, then all this stuff is important for a big reason. The more semantic you make your content now, the closer its markup will get us to this future—and the more cool stuff like this your content will be capable of.

Now who doesn't want that?

# The Lowdown on Markdown

Just because your content needs markup, that doesn't mean you or those working in your content management system necessarily need to be able to write it, or even that you must use separate fields to distinguish every little bit of content from the others.

Instead, some organizations are experimenting with crafting their content in markdown—a lightweight alternative to using HTML to give content shape that was created by John Gruber of Daring Fireball fame. Unlike full HTML, markdown allows authors to write in a standardized but natural language that can be easily read and understood not just by computers, but by humans as well.

For example, instead of the <h1> tag used in HTML, you can simply use a single hash mark to denote a heading:

```
# This text is an H1
```

Meanwhile, subheadings are made just by adding additional hash marks, like so:

```
## This text is an H2
##### This text is an H5
```

No need to close brackets or fuss with backslashes. Writing markdown is quick and simple, and is often used by people authoring common content types like blog posts.

How can something as simple as markdown help get you to markup, though? Take Portland, Oregon–based mobile startup Cloud Four, where co-founder and developer Lyza Gardner started by playing with markdown for the firm's own website, and then began exploring how it could be used for clients' content as well.

As a developer, Gardner likes markdown because it takes away all her crutches and forces her to write semantically. If she were working directly in the code, she could add non-semantic cheats to get content to do what she wants: a <div> tag here, a float there. But then those elements, which give her what she wants right now, would end up muddying her database forever. Instead, when she writes in markdown, everything she does ends up completely semantic, without it being a burden to write.

Designed specifically for writing, not publishing, markdown doesn't take the place of HTML. Instead, it has a smaller, simpler syntax associated with it—a syntax that's all about writing text, rather than doing everything that HTML can do. But if you want to include an element that doesn't exist in markdown's syntax, you can simply start writing in HTML and markdown will understand.

In addition to keeping devs like Gardner from filling their content with code cheats rather than semantic solutions, markdown is also appealing to those who want to avoid checking long lists of CMS boxes and filling out endless fields. After all, it can be easier to add some markdown to a document and push it through the system than to go through five different editing screens for a piece of content.

Even better, markdown doesn't have to stay markdown. Designed for conversion to other formats, it can easily be turned into any kind of markup language you need with one of a handful of automatic programs. In fact, Gardner has built markdown-to-CMS plug-ins for some of her clients, making it fast and efficient for users to author in markdown and have their content automatically make it into a CMS like Drupal.

Are all content authors ready to start writing in markdown? My gut says no. While human-readable, it's a big step for folks still tied tightly to working in Microsoft Word. But many—especially those with writing and editing backgrounds, like journalists or editorial staff—could be, with a little training.

That training just might start with you, dear reader—the person who's been thinking about structure and who can bridge the gap between the code and the content person who's learning to publish more effectively online.

Markdown makes a lot of sense, but it's no panacea to our content problems. Because it's so stripped down, it doesn't allow you to do things like select from a closed taxonomy or include descriptive metadata. It's also not designed to create true content "chunks," such as breaking out summaries or teasers away from the rest of the content. However, there are also an increasing number of extensions that add additional capabilities to markdown, some of which even allow markdown documents to house some forms of metadata.

In short, markdown isn't some holy grail. It's just one way smart people are trying to separate their content from its presentation, and make getting clean, easily stored content online more efficiently. But, for projects with many content types and lots of inherent structure, it may not be enough—at least, not yet.

## Many Ways to Get to Markup

Meanwhile, other organizations are trying completely different approaches, some of which don't even seem to have a lot of structure at first glance. Take West Virginia University, a public higher education institution with more than 30,000 students. With countless departments and programs making endless updates to more than two dozen different websites, the university's online presence is effectively in the hands of hundreds of people...and many of them highly unlikely to have—or want—training in creating effective digital content.

For years, these fragmented CMS users created even more fragmented content, like faculty listings that were hard-coded and had to be manually updated to add or remove names. So while preparing for a major site and CMS overhaul, what's a future-focused team to do? Crack down and insist on content processes that make markup easy? Fight the good fight, even when distributed departments don't want to? Create endless CMS forms?

Instead, the team took a more experimental approach. Rather than asking CMS users to enter content into complex form fields, they are building a system that allows them to edit pages as they appear on the desktop site, literally the same view an end user gets. An editor types content into the page's editable areas—a headline here, body content there, an address over on the right, etc.—and hits save. Once that content is saved, it's mapped back to a structured database. Based on the page template that was used, the database knows the content type. Based on how the template's fields were mapped, the database knows that a faculty member's name, bio, and contact information were entered. And the CMS user? He simply knows that his page looks like he wants.

From there, that structured content can then be used to automatically update directory listings and other related and reusable content, without worrying the author over all the details.

It's not without its problems, of course. WVU knows it can't get as specific with structure as some people might want with this approach. But it's confident that it's a step in the right direction, considering that to date, nearly every update—including updating the directory listings *and* a profile page separately when a new faculty member joins campus—has been made manually. It's also difficult to validate certain kinds of content this way, like ensuring that the text entered in a field mapped back to "phone number" in the database actually *was* a phone number.

The team at WVU has thought about all these weaknesses and more. But, for them, it's giving them a shot at creating structured content and using semantic markup—which is so much more than they've ever had before.

# The Secret to Markup

OK, here it is: There is none. The fact is, it depends—on your project, your priorities, your publication channels, and your purpose. While there's good reason to want to standardize, getting religious about which one is "right" is likely less than productive.

The good part of all that? It might matter less than you think, especially if you're working with the content itself. Because more than any specific markup type, you simply need content that's capable of being marked up: content with clear structure and chunks that are based on meaning, not presentation. And, if you've been following the course of this book, you're already on the way to having those figured out.

Also exciting is that more and more, the markup itself can be added after the fact with systems that can translate between different types of markup, seamlessly moving content stored in XML into an API that uses JSON, for example.

Speaking of APIs, that's what's next. In Chapter 7, we'll take a brief dive into the API world to understand more about what they are, how they can help get your content where it needs to go, and what content strategists, writers, IAs, and others on the nontechnical side of the spectrum need to know to make them successful.

# CHAPTER 7

# Making Sense of Content APIs

| | |
|---|---|
| What Is a Content API? | 110 |
| Content APIs in Practice | 111 |
| Why API? | 115 |
| API Approaches | 115 |
| Scoot Up to the API Table | 117 |
| Putting It All Together | 117 |

I'm not an API expert—and this chapter won't make you one, either. But as you prepare content for multiple destinations, I've found it's helpful to get a bit more comfortable with the technology that's quite likely to transport it.

In this chapter, we'll step away from our focus on the content itself for a brief discussion of APIs, or application programming interfaces: what they are, how they can make content go further, and what those of us in content strategy, IA, and related fields need to know to help make it happen.

## What Is a Content API?

Imagine this: your organization or client is coming out with a new product. The information about that product will need to be added to places like:

- The products section of the main website
- A microsite built for this line of products that's used by sales reps at trade shows
- An iOS application
- An Android application
- The product catalog
- The parent company's website
- Major retailers' ecommerce sites

How will all that content make it everywhere it needs to go? More and more often, the best answer is via a content API.

A content-focused API is, in many ways, the same as any other API. Just like the Google Maps API allows Google content to be used on lots of non-Google websites, a content-driven API stores data in a central place where other services can access and use it. After all, content is data, too.

There's just one key difference. Unlike many other types of data, like the precise latitude and longitude used in Google Maps, content—with its rich descriptions, complex narratives, and conceptual ideas—can be highly ambiguous to the machines that drive APIs. Without context and human attention, its meaning is much more difficult to parse.

Which is exactly why APIs are so important for "content people" to consider—because before content can be sent out over an API, it must get into that API. So the better we are at designing the content that goes in—which then influences the shape of the API itself—the more equipped our computers will be to process it effectively and meaningfully.

Not familiar with APIs? Well, these little acronyms play a big part in the way today's Web services work. Simply put, an API is an interface through which two computer applications can talk to one another and extract data, and they've been increasingly critical since organizations like eBay started using them back around the year 2000.

Because they allow a site to run off of data from multiple sources—and allow one piece of data to be used by as many websites or services as want or need it—APIs enable "mash-ups" and data integrations that weren't possible before. APIs allow organizations to do things like embed Google Maps in a store locator, automatically post Tweets to Facebook, embed LinkedIn job listings on a niche career site, and so much more.

APIs are built with all sorts of specifications governing which data is shared and what may be done with it, and they serve many purposes—including creating a way for content to be accessed by multiple parties and displayed on many sites and products. We're focusing on content distribution and publishing here, but you can find a lovely introduction to all kinds of APIs written for those of us without an engineering background in *APIs: A Strategy Guide* from Daniel Jacobson, Greg Brail, and Dan Woods.

Surprise, surprise: all that work you've already put in, analyzing content, structuring it meaningfully, and improving the way your CMS stores it? It's that attention and care that will allow your content API to perform.

To give you a frame of reference for how a content API could be used in your organization, let's look at some examples.

# Content APIs in Practice

All sorts of organizations use content-focused APIs, and new ones are cropping up every day. Here are just a few industries and organizations that have blazed the trail toward publishing everywhere from a central API.

## Major Media

Several major media organizations have been adopting APIs over the past few years, perhaps most notably in 2008, when both NPR and *The New York Times* announced theirs.

The *Times'* first API—released in 2008, during the throes of election season—included one simple, timely, and immensely useful type of content: presidential campaign finance data. Today, the organization's API offerings have grown to include more than a dozen types of content: movie reviews, most-popular articles, event listings, and article search, just to name a few. But that doesn't mean all *Times* content is available to anyone and everyone who requests an API key. Instead, each API offers a selection of content the *Times* is willing to share with third-party developers—for example, for the most-popular stories, API only makes titles, metadata, and links available (see Figure 7.1). If you want the rest, well, you've got to go to nytimes.com for that.

FIGURE 7.1

*The New York Times'* API for most popular news, one of the many APIs the organization offers that allows third parties to access and use *Times* content.

NPR launched its API in 2008 as well, but with a different use case in mind. Instead of wanting to open its content to third parties of all types, the organization originally wanted to get better, richer story content into the hands of its member stations, as we first learned in Chapter 2, "Building a Way Forward." But NPR quickly learned that their API would allow them to do so much more on mobile as well. In fact, the organization credits its API as the catalyst for its tremendous growth in mobile traffic, pageviews, and readership.

## Products and Shopping

It's not just publishers that can benefit from a content-driven API. In fact, retailers have been using them to share shopping content across sites for more than a decade.

When you think about it, products are an obvious example of structured content at work: each item consists of multiple elements—like the product's name, description, images, price, and available sizes or colors, just to name a few. That information gets organized into databases that help companies process orders and track inventory, so it's no surprise that retailers long ago figured out how to use this structured content to publish their product content online and across multiple sites.

For example, Zappos—the online retail store known for fast free shipping and an incredible selection of shoes and other products—uses a public API to allow developers to make use of its enormous product database. The result? Zappos content is easily integrated into things like shopping result aggregators and price comparison sites.

Meanwhile, Netflix uses an API to deliver both streaming video and the content that supports it—like titles, descriptions, genres, casts, and a whole host of metadata users rely on to search and select films and shows—to a wide range of devices, from TVs to smartphones to its iPad app, as shown in Figure 7.2.

FIGURE 7.2
Netflix pushes its collection of programming content—like descriptions of movies, series, and episodes—out to multiple platforms via its API.

## Government and Education

When you think about organizations managing big, messy content, you might think about government agencies and higher education institutions—large, decentralized entities with many departments creating and publishing many kinds of information, from research reports to news to forms. These organizations are also now turning to APIs to make content more portable, personalized, and flexible.

For example, FCC.gov—the website of the Federal Communications Commission—got an overhaul in late 2011, and the changes were much more than skin deep. In addition to a fresh design, the commission launched substantial new features designed to make its site, and the more than 250,000 pieces of content it holds, more searchable and accessible for a broad range of audiences—including frequent visitors, like telecommunications lawyers, and one-time visitors, like consumers filing a complaint.

How did the FCC do it? Via an API, of course. With help from Seabourne Consulting, which created a Drupal content API module for this project, the FCC launched the API in late 2011. Today, all of the organization's content lives in one central repository within the Drupal CMS, where it can then be published to both FCC.gov and a new beta site, my.FCC.gov, which is designed for frequent users who want to create custom dashboards of content (which we'll discuss at length in Chapter 10, "Reusable Content").

Seabourne Consulting is also designing a new mobile site for the FCC—and guess what? It'll run off the same API, but with content focused on timely information, like recent legislative updates or upcoming events—information they know mobile users want based on in-depth user research and site analytics. In fact, the API is even creating some unexpected benefits inside the FCC by powering a new cataloging system.

**TIP** DRUPAL CONTENT API

Use Drupal? Then you can use the content API designed by Seabourne Consulting, too. You'll find this open-source module at Drupal.org.

# Why API?

As you can see, organizations have widely varying reasons for adopting a content-focused API. Some, like NPR and Netflix, want to increase their reach by getting content onto more and more device-specific applications and platforms. Others, like Zappos, want their products appearing across multiple shopping sites—ideally leading to increased purchases. Still others want to use an API's structured content to power personalized content experiences, like FCC.gov. And that's just a few examples.

For any or all of these reasons, APIs can be quite powerful. And consider this: so far, many popular APIs have been created by people who aren't thinking about things like key messages and storytelling, or about user journeys and tasks—and who therefore aren't prepared to improve content's structure to support those things.

What would the possibilities be like if people like us got involved? It's time we all find out.

# API Approaches

All right, so you promise to stop fidgeting in your seat whenever the tech team starts talking in acronyms? Great. Then there are a few more things you need to know about how APIs can be designed and configured to handle content.

## Public Versus Private

When public media sends content out over the API, it increases its reach. The more people who listen or read, the better for NPR. But that isn't the case for many organizations, which want to limit their content to properties they own.

You needn't be opening your content up to the world for an API to make sense. If you want to retain some control over publishing but still want content that travels, a private API may be a much better fit for your content's future. Unlike public APIs, which developers from third parties can access and use according to the API's specifications, a private API's use is limited to those within an organization—as Netflix uses theirs—or perhaps within a limited network of partners.

In fact, many organizations have multiple APIs, some internal and some external. For example, NPR offers different APIs to different groups: a private API for those within NPR, who get the greatest flexibility in what content they can pull from the API and how they can use it; another for member stations, who receive some flexibility in terms of content and use; and a public API for external third parties like NPR Addict, which are the most limited in what content they can receive from the API. These limitations include editorial considerations—what NPR wants external parties to use—as well as legal ones, such as photo usage rights. And because the API includes rich metadata about all the content NPR produces, it's easy to filter out which content may go to whom, and when.

## Read Versus Write

You've got content and you need to get it out there, like, *right now*. So why should your API need to also accept inputs from others? Even if your primary purpose is to publish your content to the world now, the ability to allow others to write content—that is, to upload their stuff into your API—could soon be a huge boon for your business or organization.

As the number of organizations making content available via API increase, the opportunities for you to enhance and enrich your content with information from other sources—sources with content that your organization could never create or manage itself—increase as well. If your API can accept others' content, you'll be better able to create cohesive content experiences—experiences that mash the content you're really, really good at creating with the complementary stuff you'd never be able to pull off...but that your audiences want and appreciate.

Bam. Added value all around.

## What About RSS?

You may be thinking that all this talk about sending content across multiple sites sounds a lot like RSS. You're not wrong. An RSS feed is basically a simplistic API. After all, RSS stands for *real simple syndication*, and its capabilities are limited.

RSS simply makes a feed of content available to external machines, like the 10 most recent news items, for example. You set the parameters when you establish the RSS feed, and that's what the other side can receive.

An API, on the other hand, is more like a conversation between two machines: one machine makes content available. The other asks for the specific components it wants, and the first one provides them. With an API, you can slice content in different combinations, allow users to search for content, and a whole host of other things—as well as the things that RSS can do.

## Scoot Up to the API Table

When NPR launched its API back in 2008, it admits that things were imperfect: some features never caught on; some common story types weren't supported well. As the organization has revamped and improved its API over the years, it's addressed these weaknesses by making the editorial team more invested in API decisions—rather than just the engineers.

If your organization is considering or enhancing an API, there's a lesson here. When the people who know the content best are included in talks about how that content will be structured, stored, and transported, things just work better. Which means, if you've taken the time to break your content down and understand its inner workings, you're the perfect person to advocate for APIs that respect your content *and* your content creators' capabilities and constraints.

Understanding the role of the API in content distribution can also help you educate those content creators, showing them how to adjust their thinking and their workflows to be more efficient—and still create great content—in the future.

Finally, because you should be pretty much in tune with your audiences and your organization's goals by now, you'll also be prepared to help the team make decisions about what content should be available to whom, as well as how that content might need to change when the API sends it to different products, devices, or channels.

## Putting It All Together

Not everyone will need an API, true. But they're getting more difficult to avoid. Today, you may just need to publish across desktops, tablets, and smartphones, and you may find that a responsive website design does the trick just fine. But soon—if not already—you'll face even more connected devices: Internet-enabled televisions, cars, refrigerators, and thermostats, just to name a few. While responsive design can work wonders, it's not going to work for all these varied display sizes and contexts.

Instead, many organizations—media, retailers, government agencies, or any of the countless spaces in between—will need a way to transmit content that's normalized and separated from display. The better informed you are now, and the more effectively your content is structured, the more likely you are to be included in those conversations in the future.

But never forget: you can't send content *out* over your API unless you have good content going *into* your API. Which means getting content everywhere you want it still comes back to the people creating and entering it in the first place, and their ability to stop thinking about fixed pages and start thinking about building more flexible content systems—in other words, the stuff we've been working on throughout this book.

You've got the theory down. You've broken free of the page and started thinking about your content's microstructures, systems, relationships, and priorities—and you're comfortable talking about the metadata, markup, and APIs that might support them. Now it's time to embrace all the incredible places your content can go with this thinking in place.

In Part III, "Putting Structured Content to Work," we'll go from approach to application by exploring how this more flexible mindset is helping organizations of all sorts create content that's more findable, adaptable, reusable, and transportable—and how you can do the same.

# PART III

# Putting Structured Content to Work

Now that we've unlocked content from a single page or document and determined its distinct elements and parts, we have the tools to design systems that will carry it further—systems that are less linear and hierarchical, and more interconnected, contextual, and flexible. In this section, we'll explore examples of how structure is making content more findable, adaptable, reusable, and transportable—and get you excited about where your own content might go.

# CHAPTER 8

# Findable Content

More Structured, More Findable                         122
Search Engine Findability                              123
Site Search Findability                                128
Smarter Faceted Search                                 129
Related and Contextually Discoverable Content          131
Curation: The Other C-Word                             134
Finding Soul in Findability                            134

"That's *exactly* what I was looking for!"

It's a pretty good feeling, right? But as content gets unfixed and flexible and spread across all sorts of platforms, it's also a feeling too many people are missing out on, slogging their way through the muck of content farms and overgrown forests of navigation and ultimately ending up in the expansive fields of user frustration.

Thankfully, you're here to help them on this metaphor-laden journey—using your content's structure as your tool.

Don't worry: This isn't some smarmy fluff about the latest SEO techniques. It's a look at findability in many different places, both on a website and off—everything from improving what appears in search engine results to better handling site search queries, faceted search, and related or contextual content.

In this chapter, you'll see how content structure, metadata, and markup are allowing organizations to make content more findable in many different ways—and, I hope, feel inspired to consider what your own content can do.

## More Structured, More Findable

Why does structure help your content get found by your users? Ultimately, it's because it gives them so much more to find. When your content is an unstructured blob, there's only so much you can do to make the information inside accessible: You can rely on the keywords within the content to provide enough relevance for search engines to catch on; you can add generic, free-form tags to organize content; and you can build a hierarchical navigation system. And that's about it.

Once you have meaningful chunks, appropriate metadata, and content stored separate from its presentation, however, you have lots more to work with—because every attribute of the content you store can be used to increase and enhance the ways people can find it. Your metadata can support sort and filter options; your semantic markup can better inform the search engine 'bots; and your shared content attributes can link related content together. And all of this can happen without the effort, time, and expense of chasing SEO tactics or creating carefully hand-curated collections of content.

Let's look at some examples of each.

# Search Engine Findability

Search engine algorithms are constantly changing. That's partly because their robots' ability to understand content, context, and relevance is always getting better, and partly because some hucksters are constantly cooking up new ways to game the system, and the engines have to compensate for it by finding new ways to thwart them. In 2012, for example, Google released several updates designed to cut down on web-spam—many of them designed to emphasize content quality and stop over-ranking sites that engage in keyword-stuffing (repeating the same terms over and over just to game the system) and questionable linking schemes.

While lots of SEO companies out there will still sell clients on chasing the white whale of "rankings," today's world of personalized search results, social results, and constantly refreshing news means that it's near impossible to know where you "rank" on the search engine results page for any given term. Instead, you want to consider whether your content is adequately visible to—and understood by—search engines.

The good news is, by this point, you should have a lot of the work already under control. Once you've turned your content into meaningful chunks, stripped the non-semantic code from your database, and created markup that tells machines what a piece of information is, then the search-engine 'bots will have a much easier time making sense of it, too.

## Keyword-Rich Content Attributes

"What about keywords?" you might ask. Yes, they're important, but they're often mystified—like they're magical terms only an SEO guru can obtain and understand. In reality, they're simply the words your audience naturally uses when looking for your product, service, or information. If the categories and attributes you're using for your content are logical to your users, align with their mental models, and match their needs, then they'll probably match pretty closely to the terminology those same users are likely to type into a search engine, right?

You can confirm your terminology makes sense—and compare potential vocabulary choices to see what's most commonly used—with some simple research. For example, I did this back at the Arizona Office of Tourism, where we renamed a site section from "What to Do" to "Things to Do" after some analysis using keyword research tools showed that the latter phrase was a common query, while the former wasn't even on the list.

If you're new to SEO, try getting a big-picture look at how people look for your product or service online by using Google Trends (http://www.google.com/trends), which lets you compare searches over time for two or more words you think are commonly used by your audience, such as "vacation deals" versus "vacation packages." You can also get more micro information with one of many keyword research tools, where you type in a seed term and get back a range of words and phrases people commonly use. Try Wordtracker's free version (https://freekeywords.wordtracker.com) to get started.

We then used structured content and rules to relate each individual listing for various "things to do" to its appropriate city page, automatically creating plenty of content optimized for "things to do in [city name]" for all 400 or so of the state's cities—without using any of SEO's spammier gimmicks like keyword stuffing to get there. As a result, traffic from "things to do"-related keywords increased dramatically, and the user experience improved at the same time by making more valuable content accessible in more logical, useful places.

## Content Hubs

If you're working with a site where multiple content types share a single attribute—like my previous example, where businesses, hotels, parks and landmarks, feature stories, and more all shared an element for "city"—then you can also use that shared attribute to create hubs of content around a topic, much like the Sedona page we talked about earlier.

Not only can these sorts of hubs help users find things in the way they want, such as creating itineraries of things do to around Sedona, but they can also help you gain more traction with search engines. When all your content on a topic is aggregated, organized, and maybe even curated together, it creates a canonical presence: *the* place for Sedona content. Even if you have the exact same amount of content related to a topic, with the exact same keyword density—like we had all those business listings, articles, and other information spread across the site—creating a hub page can improve your SEO results substantially.

The British Broadcasting Corporation learned how beneficial this could be with BBC Food, a website dedicated to presenting the BBC's culinary content, like celebrity chefs, recipes, and food-related programs, online. With user experience designer Mike Atherton leading the way, the organization implemented what Atherton refers to as "domain-driven design"—a process not unlike the content structuring we talk about here. In this case, the BBC's content model placed the "dish" at the canonical center—like spaghetti Bolognese, for example, as shown in the screenshot in Figure 8.1. While there might be half a dozen recipes for spaghetti Bolognese, each from a different BBC-affiliated chef, there's only one dish.

By creating content hubs around each dish in the domain, the BBC was able to build a central location where users could compare various recipes, explore the chefs and shows affiliated with the dish, understand the ingredients and techniques involved, and more. Meanwhile, this page became extremely relevant for spaghetti Bolognese searches, because it was the canonical source on the topic—leading to much improved SEO results. In fact, after launching BBC Food with this approach, the site saw an increase of more than 150,000 visitors each week from search engines alone—and overall traffic doubled, from around 650,000 visitors per week to around 1.3 million.

Now, there's more to search engines—and to SEO—than structured content. But if you want to improve your visibility in search for the long haul, without sacrificing user experience or spending tons of budget on SEO consultants, then properly structured, semantic content is a great place to start.

FIGURE 8.1
The spaghetti Bolognese page from BBC Food, the center of the site's domain model. From here, you can find all spaghetti Bolognese recipes, as well as additional contextual information.

*From 2007 to 2011, London-based UXer Mike Atherton served as an information architect for the BBC, where he focused on using domain-driven design to make the media organization's seemingly endless archives of content more findable and contextually relevant for the British public. He answered a few of my questions about the role domain-driven design can play in making content work harder.*

**You're known for the term "domain-driven design." Can you define that?**

Domain-driven design is a technique borrowed from software engineering, where it's used to express complex business logic by defining the entities in a subject domain and the relationships between them. For content strategists and information architects, it's a way of saying "What are the 'things' that my content talks about and how do those things join up in the real world?"

I typically express this by sketching a domain model: a simple entity-relationship diagram where the boxes are the "things" within your subject and the arrows are all the connections between those things. As we shift toward a cross-channel, multiplatform publishing model, it helps to think about the structure of, and links between, content abstractly—rather than how those things are expressed in a particular user interface.

**What skills do we need to have to embrace domain-driven design?**

IA has its roots in taxonomic library science, where a book had to be classified in a particular way to live on one specific shelf. On the Web, this resulted in hierarchical sitemaps, starting with broader categories that drill down to narrower content. In reality, the roots and branches of knowledge are richer and more intertwined, and things don't always fall into neatly classified categories. Domain-driven design celebrates this and offers a graph structure where the connections between concepts are themselves informative. Probably the biggest mindset shift for UXers is to stop thinking about pages and page types, and instead think purely about the mental model of the subject you're trying to represent.

### How do linked data and Semantic Web fit in?

Where once we built ourselves silos on the Web, these days it pays to recognize that it's really one Web and we're in the business of stitching our content into that wider canvas. Initiatives like the Linked Open Data and Semantic Web projects are helping us do this by providing standardized methods of sharing data for both people and computers.

For example, dbPedia and MusicBrainz provide free, crowd-sourced sources of content and business data you can use to enrich and enhance your own offerings, on a scale that few businesses would have the time and resources to replicate. Conversely, by publishing out your own content in machine-readable formats like RDF, you can extend your reach by making it easier for third parties to create new and unexpected mash-ups.

### Domain-driven design also led to great SEO results for the BBC. Why is that?

The first rule of SEO is always to make great content that people want to visit and link to. Domain-driven design focuses this effort on building a page for each discrete topic in the model. This means that sites have rich internal link density, which is great for Google. But more than that, it increases the likelihood that your pages are at a level of granularity that will match search queries.

Exposing each topic resource at a single URL also makes it easier for people to link to your content when referencing that topic, much as they do with Wikipedia. This greatly boosts external link density, which in turn boosts your PageRank. SEO isn't black magic—it's just making great stuff that people can easily link to, and domain-driven design helps accomplish that.

*Mike Atherton writes about domain-driven design and other user experience–related topics at* reduxd.com.

# Site Search Findability

Often overlooked by both UXers and content strategists, improving the performance of your own site's search engine—that is, how easily and accurately your users find the information they want using it—is frequently a simple way to glean immediate improvements to a website's performance.

Site search data is powerful stuff: it tells you, in users' own words, what they want from your site and whether or not you have it. By analyzing what your users are typing in, you can see whether there are things they want that you don't have, confirm whether they're getting results to their common queries, and—most importantly for this book—make sure the results they're finding are the most appropriate, relevant ones.

**TIP** GETTING STARTED WITH SITE SEARCH

> For a deep dive into your site search data, pick up *Search Analytics for Your Site: Conversations with Your Customers* by Lou Rosenfeld, also published by Rosenfeld Media.

Once you start analyzing your site search data, you'll probably find a whole list of ways you'd like to adjust your search engine's performance to better meet searchers' needs. Lo and behold, the better your content is structured, the easier it will be to implement these recommendations.

Remember how we talked about building rules in Chapter 5, "Designing Content Systems"? Well, when you really look at it, your site's internal search engine just uses another set of rules, combing your site's content and deciding what the most relevant response to a query should be. And unlike external search engines like Google or Bing, you can change the way your site's search engine works, prioritizing some factors and deprioritizing others in ways that help the right content bubble up to the surface.

Just like with external search engines, when your content is stored in modular parts, you're essentially giving your internal search engine more to work with: more chunks, more labels that help it understand what a piece of content is about. But structured content does something even greater for internal site search: it gives you lots of easy ways to tune your search engine results systematically.

One way you might tune results is by content type. For example, while working with a large university, I found that certain types of content, like press releases, were showing up disproportionately frequently in top search results—even when those press releases were several years old, and the query was something general and immediate, like "dorm costs." Overall, we saw that users' queries tended to map to a need for immediate information, not historical facts—and because press releases represent a moment in time, they were unlikely to meet this need. Likely at least in part due to this, the number of users who were abandoning the site after seeing a search results page was extremely high.

Tuning search engine performance takes careful attention and a bit of tweaking, but in this case, it was easy to decrease the weight for press releases as a whole—meaning they would still show up in search results, and could even be at the top of the pile for more specific queries where their content seemed especially relevant, but they were much less likely to make it to the top for most general terms.

In addition to prioritizing or deprioritizing whole content types, having content structured into meaningful chunks also allows you to put more or less weight on different elements of content. For example, if you have summaries or abstracts associated with all your content, those fields could be given greater weight in determining search engine relevance—the reasoning being, if it's in the abstract, then that keyword must *really* be central to that piece of content, not just tangentially referenced. Or, you might find that you want to prioritize articles or other content that's been recently published, and deprioritize content that's older—something that's much easier to do if your content is structured.

Without structure behind your content, your internal site search will rely on what it can glean from a large content block—in other words, relatively little. This means to tune it to your needs, you'll typically be less able to make changes to its algorithm—the equation that consistently governs how content relevance is weighted—and instead rely more on hacks: overrides to the algorithm's logic. And while those hacks are OK here and there, they're a manual fix: While you can likely implement them for a few highly searched terms, you could do more to benefit the entire site search engine if you put some structure behind it.

## Smarter Faceted Search

Faceted search, which allows users to sort and filter content using multiple criteria, has been around for years—perhaps most notably on online shopping sites, where you can whittle product results down to those most relevant to your search with criteria like size, color, brand, and price. It's incredibly helpful, and perhaps even necessary, for navigating large product inventories. Could you imagine shopping Zappos, the online retailer of shoes and other apparel, without it? Even a search for a relatively specific item—a pair of black peep-toe heels, for example—can return hundreds of products (see Figure 8.2).

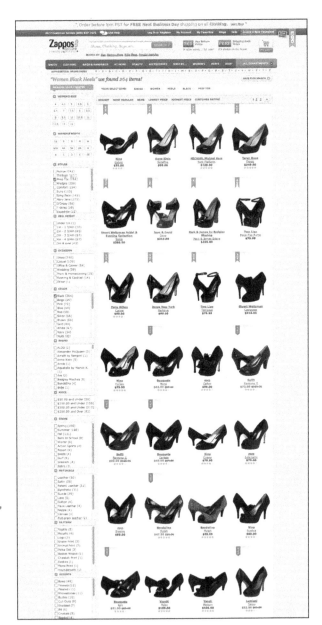

FIGURE 8.2
Navigating product sites, like Zappos.com, would be near impossible without faceted search, which is powered by structured content—but would benefit other types of content as well.

What online retail figured out long ago is that users wanted to find products in different ways, accessing and ordering products differently depending on their unique requirements or desires, rather than being forced to scroll through all items in a predetermined order set by the site. What the industry also figured out was that this level of faceted search requires structure—because in order to sort or filter by a certain criterion, that element must exist in a separate spot in the database.

Because of this, product listings for shopping are now nearly always structured, and their format is relatively consistent across different sites—making it possible for all kinds of things to work, from Google search results extracting the price of a product you search for without you even clicking through to view it, to those shopping aggregators that allow you to compare multiple sites' deals on the same product.

Not all kinds of content need this level of personal control over sorting and filtering, of course. But if you have lots of content that's designed for exploring—think things like recipes, help articles, restaurant listings, and anything else people might want to parse in different ways—you can put your content elements to work to help your users avoid a frustrating needle-in-a-haystack experience.

## Related and Contextually Discoverable Content

When I first started working with websites—at the time, for a marketing-focused group obsessed with SEO, lead forms, and conversion rates—it seemed like every single sidebar we recommended was the same: an exposed lead form or a big call to action to buy now.

Needless to say (or maybe not, since I still see so many of them out there), these super-salesy sidebars don't always work so well—because they didn't take into account what users actually wanted to do next.

In other places, you see related or contextually accessible content all the time: links to additional articles at the bottom of a story, for example, or similar dishes along the sidebar of a recipe page. But how often is this content actually relevant?

These sidebars and related items lists are often based on free-form keyword tags or automatically generated lists—creating relationships that are assumed, rather than inherent to the content itself. As Atherton found when working with the BBC, this makes for a weak relationship. But when you have structure behind your content, such as with domain modeling, you create an ontological relationship—one built at the deepest level of the content, cutting to the core of its "thingness," the stuff that makes the content what it is. This ensures related and contextual information is actually deeply rooted to the topic of the page—no questionable keywords required.

One easy-to-understand example of these deep relationships in action is the BBC's Wildlife Finder. Because the BBC—and, by extension, much of the British public, who fund the BBC by paying television licensing fees—had invested substantially in creating a vast amount of nature video, the organization wanted to get more mileage out of this content than simply creating massive archives. The team took on the challenge by building a system for relating contextually relevant information based off a well-known historic domain: the Linnaean taxonomy, otherwise known as the animal classification system.

With this, you can visit a page about a specific animal, like the cheetah (shown in Figure 8.3), and from there, easily find videos, news, and links related to cheetahs. In addition, the structured classification system also opens up a wide range of related content options: a quick link up a level allows you to explore the entire felidae (cat) family, while a selection of related animals creates a parallel for exploring similar species, like the lynx.

In addition to using animal classification to structure BBC Wildlife content, the team also derived a system that included other information about animals, including their habitats and behaviors. For example, from the panda page, you can see that a panda lives in a broadleaf forest. By clicking through to the broadleaf forest page, you can see what a broadleaf forest means, as well as what other sorts of animals live there. And all these pages of content are built automatically, using the content's underlying structure to dictate what's contextually relevant where.

Finally, remember our introduction to linked data in Chapter 6, "Understanding Markup"? Well, the BBC is making use of that, too. Rather than, say, hiring writers to craft overviews of every animal the BBC has video footage about, the organization relies on content from other sources, accessible via linked data. That is, by structuring content along the same lines as sources like Wikipedia, the BBC can automatically pull in the content it doesn't have—and isn't invested enough in to create—from an external source.

FIGURE 8.3
BBC Wildlife's collection of cheetah-related content and links to other animals, habitats, and more—all pulled together automatically based on their content's structure.

# Curation: The Other C-Word

Content curation has been a buzzword for a few years now, and it's no wonder. As many sites move toward content hubs and lists of related links like the BBC's wildlife pages, more than a few have started referring to their efforts as curation.

Problem is, curation is a complicated, often contentious thing. While some marketeers call all automated lists of links "curated," folks from museums and other curatorial roles often find it more than a little unsettling to see a term from their highly specialized fields appropriated so readily.

In a museum setting, curators do much more than collect like things and put them in a room together. They examine cultural trends or historical objects and extract themes, movements, and influences. They arrange works in a way that highlights and contrasts, or that throws viewers' assumptions into relief. They select pieces that are individually interesting, but that together tell an even richer story.

In short: curation makes new meaning—it creates something that's more than the sum of its parts.

Curation is also a very human act—one that requires careful attention, editorial sensibility, storytelling skills, and a finely tuned sense of cultural relevance. It can be seen online in people like Jason Kottke and Maria Popova, who weave together some of the most interesting tidbits they find with their own commentary and cultural footnotes, connecting readers to ideas, art, stories, and more. The robots just can't manage all that yet (whether we ever want them to is, perhaps, another story). While each is valuable in its own right, it's quite a reach to equate any of the automated approaches discussed here with true curatorial care.

# Finding Soul in Findability

One of the biggest benefits to structured content could also become its greatest pitfall. As it gets easier to automatically compile lists of links that are relevant to a topic, or to allow users to search through data in seemingly endlessly faceted ways, there's a risk that the experience can become robotic: that the resulting content experiences will be reduced to data, not meaningful stories, information, and ideas. It's hard to make an automated link list memorable.

While structured content and automatically generated pages may not have the power and nuances of curation, this approach to related, contextual, findable content does offer much more than a basic content aggregation system. By designing content models that fit your users' own mental models for how information connects and makes meaning, you can design a system that relies on a sort of human-influenced robotic editing—resulting in a collection of information created automatically, yes, but that is informed by human care and understanding. It will never offer the handcrafted, carefully culled experience a fantastic human editor can provide. But it's a start toward efficiently building collections of content that are more thoughtful, useful, and thematic.

After all, you don't have the time, resources, or money to apply that level of care to every piece of content in the universe, particularly if you're trying to make a large repository of information useful, like the BBC did with its archives. Instead, by allowing the robots to do some of the work—and giving them the well-structured content they need to do their work well—you can save your precious human capital for the most important, valuable content.

# CHAPTER 9

# Adaptable Content

| | |
|---|---|
| Looking Beyond Layout | 139 |
| Intermixing Content | 141 |
| Content Layering | 143 |
| Removing Content | 145 |
| Making Content Lightweight | 147 |
| Simplicity from the Start | 148 |
| Adding Content | 150 |
| Responsibly Responsive | 151 |

If you've paid any attention to the Web the past couple years, chances are you've heard a lot of opinions about responsive and adaptive design—from the fawning to the illuminating to, occasionally, the nay-saying. Amid all the hype, though, one thing is clear: we need websites that users can access from a range of devices with a range of capabilities—and these approaches are one way to get there.

While this trend often seems like a design-and-dev problem, it's much more than that—because all this reshaping and reflowing gives plenty for us content wonks to consider as well, as we first touched on in the Starbucks example in Chapter 5, "Designing Content Systems." From which content takes priority to how different elements combine into a single column, responsive and adaptive designs put our content challenges front and center, making it harder than ever to hide messy content behind pretty designs.

**TIP** RESPONSIVE OR ADAPTIVE?

While responsive and adaptive designs have a lot in common—including many of the same content considerations—these two terms are not quite interchangeable. Adaptive design is a more general term, denoting all the things you can do to make an interface adapt to a user's device. It's often seen as an extension of progressive enhancement—the concept that a site's core functionality works on even the most basic devices, and the experience gets progressively better on those devices that can accommodate it. Adaptive design, then, can include many things, including changes to markup and JavaScript and support for assistive technology devices. Responsive design, on the other hand, implies a more specific set of practices: fluid grids, fluid images, and media queries that allow a site to reflow gracefully for different screen sizes. For more, check out Aaron Gustafson's book, *Adaptive Web Design,* and Ethan Marcotte's *Responsive Web Design*, the seminal titles on both subjects.

In this chapter, we'll give these and other issues around content for responsive and adaptive experiences a closer look—and see how we can use these approaches to make the most of our content.

# Looking Beyond Layout

> Media-queried responsive and adaptive sites afford us the ability
> to re-architect content on a page to fit its container, but with this
> exciting new potential come equally exciting challenges. Web
> designers will have to look beyond the layout in front of them to
> envision how its elements will reflow and lockup at various widths
> while maintaining form and hierarchy.
>
> —Trent Walton[1]

Walton, a designer and partner in Texas-based firm Paravel, may have written this post for other designers, but it hits at the heart of what we're trying to accomplish with structured, well-architected content as well: to move beyond the limitations of pages and documents and start embracing the content itself—in whatever form it needs to be displayed.

In this way, adaptive and responsive design provide the perfect backdrop for rethinking your content. Because as you stop being able to dictate precisely where a piece of information will be displayed on a given page, you're forced to instead start thinking in terms of systems and packages of information—packages that could look different depending on where and how they're being viewed.

Of course, things were never actually fixed and immutable. Even during those brief sweet years after Web standards took off but before people started trading in their desktops for mobile devices, you never *really* knew what a user's display would look like. Low bandwidth, accessibility devices, old monitors, outdated browsers, and myriad other circumstances could easily turn your perfectly crafted experience into something that looked radically different.

Back then, it was simply easier to pretend otherwise—to act as if every element on a page was super-glued into place. After all, if you worked online, you were pretty likely to have a modern desktop machine and a decent Internet connection, so you might never see how your site looked to those in less desirable circumstances.

Now, those alternate realities are difficult to avoid, even for those of us who immediately adopt all the latest gadgets and have endless budget for bandwidth: whether you're spying a site on an iPhone or attempting to book tickets on some hotel's interminably slow Wi-Fi, odds are good you'll face a less-than-desirable experience pretty regularly.

---

1   http://rfld.me/MhSooY

While responsive and adaptive design is still relatively new—and practitioners are developing smart additions and tweaks to their methodologies nearly every day—Walton's vision for content has begun to become reality, as have a number of other approaches to handling content in smart, flexible, appropriate ways. Let's dive into a few of them.

## Emerging CSS Specs for Flexible Content

Designers and developers working to build responsive and adaptive layouts have recently been lamenting some of the technical challenges with making content flex and flow in smart, useful ways. But a couple different CSS specifications are gaining adoption and starting to change that: flexbox and grid layouts. Here's what content-focused folks ought to know about both:

**Flexbox,** which is short for Flexible Box Layout Module, is a CSS working draft that allows you to create and nest flexible boxes of content on a page, allowing for visual layouts that are more complex. It also offers source-order independence, which means you can change the order of items on the page for different layouts—something that comes in handy when trying to either keep your intended content priority intact when screen size narrows, or to introduce a new priority of content for specific device types.

**Grid layouts,** on the other hand, divide space into columns and rows. From there, you can make decisions about how those predictably sized spaces change for different display sizes, so you can have just one set of semantic markup, but use media queries to rearrange the order and placement of different content elements.

Both of these solutions are still considered working drafts—as are many of the approaches designers and developers rely on regularly—which means they're not yet supported by all browsers, and they are still undergoing changes and debate.

Ultimately, some of these technical issues around making content more adaptable will be resolved—perhaps even by the time you're reading this book. Once removed, the much bigger hurdle will be the content: whether it has the back-end structure to allow for logical layout shift, without manual intervention.

By structuring and storing content in smarter ways now, you'll be much more prepared for whatever technical implementation is needed, which means you'll launch better sites more quickly.

# Intermixing Content

Letting go of control is scary, but there's also a beauty in looking beyond lay-out—in dismantling notions about pages and documents. When you do, you uncover something messier, but also quite powerful: meaning.

But many of the responsive websites you see today simply stack their content, slipping sidebars below "main" content like in our Starbucks example in Chapter 5, rather than taking their meaning and message into account. While this solution is more usable and useful than doing nothing for your mobile customers, it's a one-size-fits-all approach—and one I think we can do better than.

Thankfully, there's another way to think about shifting content for varied screen sizes: intermixing it, or what Trent Walton refers to as "interdigitation." When you interdigitate content, you fold it in, weaving bits of one piece of content in between parts of another, rather than just plopping it to the bottom of the page, as shown in Figure 9.1.

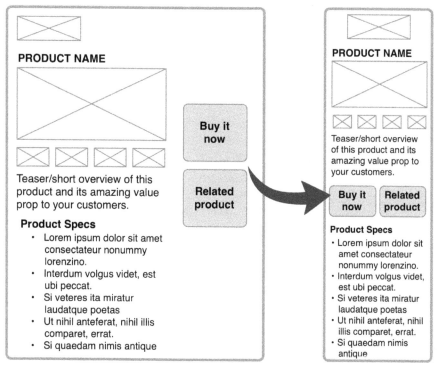

FIGURE 9.1

An example of how product content might reflow at small screen sizes. When you interdigitate content, key elements, like calls to action, can retain their emphasis at any display size.

When dealing with several smaller content modules that need to coexist alongside a longer one—such as relating a quick facts sidebar to a long feature story, or featuring a food product you sell alongside the recipe in which it's used—you might find that simply allowing those small little modules to end up below a long, involved content piece throws off the story, displaces useful information, or otherwise breaks the user's ability to understand, use, or enjoy the content.

Instead, interdigitating the content allows you to keep the narrative, persuasive, or informational structure of the content intact by placing content pieces where they make sense, in between the longer bits, thus offering valuable and useful information at the right time.

One place this sort of thinking has been implemented is the *Boston Globe*'s responsive site, which launched in the fall of 2011 to great anticipation (and perhaps even greater praise). One of the first large-scale responsive sites to launch, the project required the team—which included Ethan Marcotte and the folks at Filament Group—to think about how complex content would work in an experience that was also ad-supported. That is, while the new bostonglobe. com is all about showcasing premium journalism, it can't do it at the expense of those paying to appear there. Shuffling advertising content to the end of a story, at the bottom of the page, below a story, certainly wasn't a solution for small screens.

Instead, Filament Group developed a JavaScript approach that has since been polished up and shared with the world as AppendAround. It works like this: You create multiple containers in different sizes for each chunk of content you have, and then configure your CSS to only display one container for each content chunk at a time. As a result, a piece of content can easily change its location or priority at different screen sizes, depending on which container it's told to use.

This solution worked well for the *Globe*'s advertising, as shown in Figure 9.2. But it's also a way to get other kinds of content to move around the page to meet your strategic priorities and user needs—if you have modular content, that is.

FIGURE 9.2
Advertising appears in the right-hand sidebar on the desktop version of the new Boston Globe site, but is reconfigured to tuck between elements as you scroll down the page in the smartphone-sized version.

# Content Layering

Remember how we saw Starbucks' responsive design place long-form copy and a whole mess of reviews above the button to buy coffee—as well as its critical tasting notes? Well, one way folks are looking to solve this problem is with layering content for smaller screens, making some items minimized—but easily expandable—in order to keep the page manageable for skimming and scrolling.

Take the University of Notre Dame, which launched a new responsive version of ND.edu in early 2012, as shown in Figure 9.3. On desktops and tablets, main content areas like "About" and "Academics" are anchor-linked sections on the homepage, available by either using the navigation or simply scrolling down the homepage. But on smartphones, as shown in Figure 9.4, that content is tucked into interior pages—clearly available, but just a click away—to keep the homepage a bit more manageable.

FIGURE 9.3
On larger screen sizes, the University of Notre Dame's main navigation anchor links to content further down the homepage, like the "About" section shown here (the rest of the items scrolled too far down to include in this shot).

**FIGURE 9.4**
In contrast to Figure 9.3, on the iPhone, Notre Dame's "About" section is layered a level deeper, on its own page, rather than anchor-linked on the homepage.

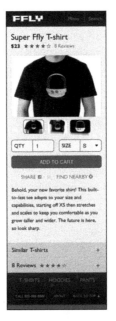

**FIGURE 9.5**
Brad Frost's future-friendly demo site, showing some of the latest mobile capabilities. See how review content is obviously available, yet tucked a tap away instead of taking over the entire page.

Mobile designer and developer Brad Frost has been working on similar ways to layer some content for small screens with a demo project, which he's calling the Future Friendly online store—a fake ecommerce site. Here, reviews (which we saw take up reams and reams of space on the Starbucks site) are cleverly tucked into an expandable area, with only the overall star rating and number of reviews for each item visible at first, as you can see in Figure 9.5.

In this example, Frost uses an approach called an AJAX include pattern for modular content that allows the site to conditionally load content—that is, to load mandatory content quickly in a lightweight manner that doesn't rely on JavaScript, something not all devices can support. That experience is then enhanced with nice-to-have features on more capable devices, without slowing down the initial page load.

What makes this approach work is that content isn't missing or hard to find; it's right there, where you'd expect it—just behind an easy tap. Given that a study from Google at the end of 2010 found that 70 percent of smartphone owners say they use their phones in stores to help make purchase decisions,[2] keeping product reviews easy to find and quick to skim seems like a logical move. And because key information is pulled out—the number of reviews and average rating—many users likely won't even need to see more. Those who do want detail, or who are looking for answers to specific questions, can easily get it.

Much of this sort of solution relies on how the page is designed and developed, but there's a clear reason for content and IA folks to be included in these discussions—because you can help make smart decisions about how much content (and which bits) can reasonably be tucked away behind a tap, versus which ones need to be expanded at all times.

Of course, in order to layer content, that content needs to be structured—written and stored in such a way that parts can be exposed and parts hidden based on business rules and conditions. Typically, this happens pretty naturally with reviews, because reviews are submitted one at a time, so each review necessarily ends up stored separately. But what other types of content could you organize in this way, if you had structure behind them?

## Removing Content

"No one will ever want to do *that* on their phone!"

Sound familiar? You may have heard it a lot in discussions about mobile, but the truth is, people do all kinds of things on all kinds of devices—sometimes out of necessity, sometimes convenience, sometimes preference. And it's really hard to anticipate when, where, or how they'll want to do it.

In fact, as of February 2012, nearly half of all Americans owned a smartphone, according to a Pew Internet research report—up from only one in three just 10 months prior to that date. And according to a 2011 Pew report, about one-fourth of those who own smartphones use them as their primary Internet access device—and this is particularly true in low-income populations.[3]

2  http://rfld.me/QjTkI9

3  Read the Pew 2012 Digital Differences report at http://rfld.me/NT3e23 and the 2011 Smartphones report at http://rfld.me/QbP522.

In light of this landscape, it's nearly impossible to say what a user will or won't want to do from her mobile device. We've all seen people browse websites while watching TV, settle bets at the bar with a quick Wikipedia lookup, or pay bills and play games during a long flight layover. Luke Wroblewski has noted that thousands of cars are purchased on eBay using mobile devices each week.[4] Hell, there's probably even a person out there reading a Russian novel while standing in an interminable DMV line right now.

The more you assume what people will and won't want or need, the more you put artificial limitations on your content—limitations you're going to have to undo later, when smartphone ownership reaches total saturation and your user population simply demands it.

Take our example of ASU Online from Chapter 1, "Framing the New Content Challenge." When the ASU team started working with Happy Cog, it had a hard time believing anyone would apply for college on a smartphone. They were wrong. Once the site functioned well on mobile devices, admissions applications from smartphone users started rolling in.

It's precisely this that makes responsive and adaptive design so powerful: because it allows us to serve users complete content in a way that feels unified with, even when different from, the desktop experience. And it builds trust in the experience, creating an expectation that this is not "the mobile site," but rather, *the site*.

Once you set this expectation, though, you need to deliver—not skimp on the details because you assumed no one on a smartphone would ever make it that far. That is, building a site that acts responsively, but limits the content available to mobile users, simply won't cut it.

On the other hand, if you do have a clear use case for providing mobile users profoundly different content than desktop ones, then you may have a great reason to build an app. The key difference here is that native applications—those that are installed, versus navigated to—allow users to self-identify and select services based on their needs. For example, when someone downloads the Facebook Camera app, he's saying "I want to easily take photos and post them to Facebook." When he downloads the NPR Music iPhone app, he's saying, "I want quick access to music-related content."

On the other hand, when a user simply visits your site from a smartphone, you can't be sure what he's there for—which makes limiting the content he can access from that device highly problematic. After all, a customer doesn't care what the *average user* wants on mobile. He only cares about the needs of one person: himself. That's why a site that can offer complete content on any device makes a lot of sense, and should likely be your baseline mobile offering.

---

4  Hear Wroblewski talk about this with Jared Spool at http://rfld.me/Nx5Kbl.

# Making Content Lightweight

Some types of content trimming do make sense, though—such as cutting excess fat to boost site performance. Visual content can be especially weighty, hungrily consuming your users' data connection and creating painful, frustratingly long page loads.

According to a KISS Metrics study in 2011, nearly half of mobile users expect a page to load within two seconds, and 40 percent say they'll abandon a site that doesn't load within three seconds[5]—meaning it's imperative to keep close tabs on any content that could weigh down an experience.

To accommodate this, lots of designers are implementing conditionally loading content, often called *lazy loading*, like Brad Frost did in his Future Friendly store demo: once the core content has loaded, the non-essential bits are requested using some JavaScript.

But guess what? You'll find it rather hard to conditionally load or strip out content unless the content you want to treat differently is also structured in such a way that it's extractable. If it's all in one big blob, yet again, you're stuck with very few options.

While lazy-loading content or removing some images may sometimes make sense for small screens, this approach to solving the load time problem also begs another question: Should that content be there in the first place?

Boston-based designer and developer Mat Marquis once answered that query on Twitter, tongue firmly planted in cheek: "Mobile users want to see our menu, hours, and delivery number. Desktop users definitely want this 1mb png of someone smiling at a salad."

Oftentimes, as Marquis alludes to, the stuff we cram into the desktop versions of our sites is just that: stuff. Not content that's actually communicating anything valuable or enriching our users' experiences. It's just a large, bandwidth-sucking stock photo of someone grinning blandly at a bowl of lettuce.

In this way, considering all the different devices on which your content may be displayed forces you to focus—to take stock of what's really important, and to get rid of the things that aren't. As Luke Wroblewski notes: "If you design for mobile first, you can create agreement up front on what matters most. You can then apply the same rationale to the desktop (and any other) experience of your web product."[6]

---

5  http://rfld.me/OHU5u3

6  Luke Wroblewski, *Mobile First* (New York: A Book Apart, 2011).

# Simplicity from the Start

Those who don't design for readers may soon not be designing for anyone.

—Jeffrey Zeldman[7]

The more time we spend trying to fit flashy desktop experiences onto tiny little devices, the more we must ask ourselves: What's all this stuff doing here, anyway? Do we need another sidebar? What's the point of shoveling 17 content elements into a single template? Do our users really want a thousand glittering options shoved down their throats all at once?

Whereas some mobile-optimized experiences simply eliminate the junk from small-screen applications (while leaving desktop users knee-deep in flashing banners and screen takeovers), responsive design doesn't let you off the hook so easily. Instead, because it's attempting to offer parity of experience across devices, it can force you to focus—to separate the wheat from the chaff of your content, and to allow your poor users, regardless of device, to rest their tired, abused little retinas on just one thing at a time. When you let them simply read the article, follow the directions, or experience a story, then maybe—just maybe—they'll then actually *want* to read more when they're done. No sleazy pageview-generating tactics needed.

Jeffrey Zeldman did just that in May of 2012. His long-running personal site, Zeldman.com, suddenly started sporting a single column of text, featuring a Georgia typeface displayed with surprising size on the desktop version, as shown in Figure 9.6.

Some folks cheered; some folks jeered. Zeldman himself wrote a manifesto about the subject, telling readers that is was an experiment in putting readers first, and in removing anything and everything extraneous from the page—regardless of the size of the browser on which it was being displayed.

It's a "content first" approach taken to the extreme, and one I can't help but get excited about. Of course, it's not for everyone, nor for everything. When you start stripping experiences down to their core—the content—it's critical to also remember: You are not Jeffrey Zeldman (and chances are, your client's ecommerce site or your boss' new pet project are even further removed from someone once dubbed the "King of Web Standards" by *Businessweek*). Your organization might have more complex needs than simply wanting users to read a post. And your users may well be interested in doing more than immersing themselves in a single piece of content.

---

7 http://rfld.me/MxsmcS

## WEB DESIGN MANIFESTO 2012

THANK YOU for the screen shot. I was actually already aware that the type on my site is big. I designed it that way. And while I'm grateful for your kind desire to help me, I actually do know how the site looks in a browser with default settings on a desktop computer. I am fortunate enough to own a desktop computer. Moreover, I work in a design studio where we have several of them.

This is my personal site. There are many like it, but this one is mine. Designers with personal sites should experiment with new layout models when they can. Before I got busy with one thing and another, I used to redesign this site practically every other week. Sometimes the designs experimented with pitifully low contrast. Other times the type was absurdly small. I experimented with the technology that's used to create web layouts, and with various notions of web "page" design and content presentation. I'm still doing that, I just don't get to do it as often.

Many people who've visited this site since the redesign have commented on the big type. It's hard to miss. After all, words are practically the only feature I haven't removed. Some of the people say they love it. Others are undecided. Many are still processing. A few say they hate it and suggest I've lost my mind—although nobody until you has suggested I simply didn't have access to a computer and therefore didn't know what I was designing. This design may be good, bad, or indifferent but it is not accidental.

A few people who hate this design have asked if I've heard of responsive web design. I have indeed. I was there when Ethan Marcotte invented it, I published his ground-breaking article (and, later, his book, which I read in draft half a dozen times and which I still turn to for reference and pleasure), and I've had the privilege of seeing Ethan lecture and lead workshops on the topic about 40 times over the past three years. We've incorporated responsive design in our studio's practice, and I've talked about it myself on various stages in three countries. I'm even using elements of it in this design, although you'd have to view source and think hard to understand how, and I don't feel like explaining that part yet.

This redesign is a response to ebooks, to web type, to mobile, and to wonderful applications like Instapaper and Readability that address the problem of most websites' pointlessly cluttered interfaces and content-hostile text layouts by actually removing the designer from the equation. (That's not all these apps do, but it's one benefit of using them,

**FIGURE 9.6**
Jeffrey Zeldman's redesigned website, showcasing his 2012 manifesto post where he explains the new approach. The page scrolls further, but really, this is about it: content, content, content.

Last, but most certainly not least, you may be dealing with an advertising-supported revenue model, and those advertisers aren't about to look the other way as you squeeze them further and further into the margins of your design. (And, of course, if you eliminate them entirely, they're pretty unlikely to keep paying you.) While the online advertising model has some serious problems—and deserves an analysis too detailed for the scope of this book—your redesign project may not be an effective time to try to solve them.

Ultimately, responsive design doesn't answer a single one of these questions. It only makes the questions themselves more obvious, and more necessary to start considering. Wherever the balance of your project lies—between offering readers focus or offering them options; between serving ads or serving substance—you'll have a better chance at finding it when you embrace an adaptive mindset, considering what you're trying to communicate rather than just designing the space you're going to do it in.

## Adding Content

One of the most exciting modes of thinking to come out of the mobile movement is this: while devices like tablets and smartphones can have very different capabilities, it's oversimplified to claim a modern mobile device is "less capable" than its desktop cousin. After all, can you point your desktop screen east and see which restaurants are currently open in that direction? Can your desktop guide your driving, turn by turn?

Despite their small screens, today's smartphones and other location-aware, Internet-enabled devices can also be seen as *more* capable than desktops, because they have all kinds of contextual tools built in: touch screens, accelerometers, GPS, and the like. And that means they give us the opportunity to add special features and functions that only make sense on mobile.

Because of this, mobile advocate Stephen Hay has long argued that content should be platform-agnostic—that is, everyone can access all the same content, no matter what. However, the experience itself should be platform-aware, where the device's unique capabilities are taken into account, and enhanced features are included to support them.

How might that affect your content? Well, consider the case of a university like Notre Dame, which wants to attract top students. While sweeping imagery of the lush, historic campus might help persuade a teen searching from her home to consider the school, it's not going to do much for a prospective student already on a campus visit. But you know what might help seal the deal? Convincing that student to take a group tour, where she'll gain a better feel for the university and meet some of her prospective classmates.

In fact, Notre Dame is now considering ways to help make that happen by creating location-aware features that can notify visiting prospects about upcoming tours, and then give them step-by-step directions to the tour's starting location—effectively enhancing their experience in ways that would be impossible on a traditional desktop website.

## Responsibly Responsive

Ultimately, responsive and adaptive websites aren't about guessing what users might want—or deciding what they should want—on different devices. They're about ensuring people can easily and enjoyably access whatever they need. And there's no one right way to make them work.

Whether you choose to fold in modules, collapse content elements, or strip your content assets down to essentials, your content's structure will help you—both strategically and functionally. Because you've taken a close look at your content and considered its meaning, relationships, and priorities, you're prepared to make otherwise tough decisions about what goes where, when, and why. And because you've structured and stored your content in pieces and parts, you can extract the content you need in lots of different ways, reshaping and recombining elements to create the layout that makes the most sense for all parties involved.

Best of all, your close attention to content means you've got key information your design and development team might otherwise be missing—and there's no better time to start sharing it with them, making the end result better for all parties.

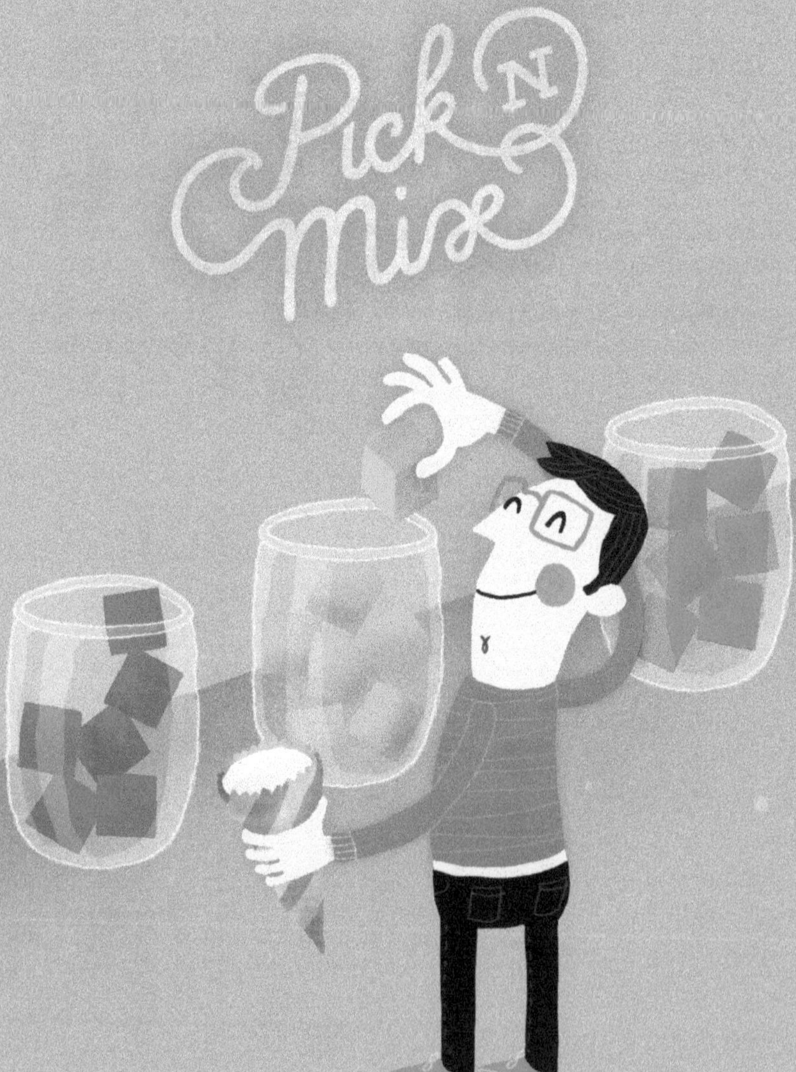
Pick N Mix

# Reusable Content

Revisiting Content Reuse                                    154

Building a Central Content Store                            155

Content Across Products                                     156

Personalized Content                                        162

A Reuse Imperative                                          163

And Now for Something Completely Different                  168

Chasing Perfection                                          170

Making Reuse Meaningful                                     171

In Chapter 9, "Adaptable Content," we learned about different considerations for content in responsive and adaptive websites. But that's just one way your content might need to shift. Like the oft-touted NPR example, you may also need to get content out across lots of very different products or destinations. Or, you might not really be dealing with publishing content all at once, but rather creating a repository of information that can be used in the future, however it's needed—or even selected and arranged by your users, creating their own personalized collections of your content to suit whatever their needs happen to be.

This is the world of reusable and reconfigurable content: content that can be pushed out lots of places at once, assembled and associated with other relevant bits on the fly, displayed in different combinations for different purposes, or connected and combined by users themselves.

In this chapter, we'll explore the ways that reuse might be useful for whatever it is your content is facing, discuss things to consider when prepping content for reuse, and, of course, see how structured content will help you at every step of the way. We'll also look at an unexpected example of content reuse and see why you don't need to have the perfect plan in place to start making your content more reusable, useful, and efficient now.

## Revisiting Content Reuse

Reusable content has been a rallying cry of the technical communications crowd for a couple decades now, and for good reason. As we touched on in Chapter 2, "Building a Way Forward," large organizations have long needed ways to make things like help content, specifications, instructions, and other technical documentation easily reusable and translatable for everything from product manuals to customer-facing websites to intranets.

For example, Ann Rockley, the CEO of consulting firm the Rockley Group, wrote the first edition of her book *Managing Enterprise Content*, which focuses heavily on content reusability, way back in 2002. In those days, there was no need for a chapter about mobile content, nor to think about responsive and adaptive experiences. But there was still plenty of practical information on how to manage content across distributed organizations by structuring it, storing it in a central database, and considering how it could be reused.

Back then, pretty much everyone talking about content structure and reuse, though, was focusing on a couple of very specific technologies: XML and DITA, which we touched on in Chapter 6, "Understanding Markup." Today, the need for reusable, reconfigurable content is no longer limited to those in huge enterprises or with strict technical requirements—and that means that as reuse goes mainstream, people are developing all sorts of new ways to make it happen, ranging from the semi-manual to the completely automated. And they're doing it in all kinds of places, even some spots where you might not expect coordinated efforts at efficiency and innovation, like the federal government.

Let's take a look at a few of them and start seeing why reusable content needn't be a pipe dream—nor is it the answer to every content problem.

# Building a Central Content Store

The documentation and knowledge management industry was probably the first to embrace reusable content, often in the form of central content stores or repositories. Content stores have long made sense for things like documentation, which might be used by everyone from customers to customer service reps to the IT team, all operating in different countries and speaking a multitude of languages.

A central content store helps by allowing authors to write information in a structured environment, and then make that information accessible to a variety of people who use it to publish a variety of different content products.

For example, consider a major electronics producer that sells personal computers and related items in countries around the world—and requires technical documentation for all of those products, in several dozen different languages.

In the past, all that work would have been done by technical writers crafting manuals in Microsoft Word, which would then make their way through the production and translation/localization process and come out the other side as final printed pieces. While these documents served their purpose well, all that content was essentially locked up: because it was created in large, single documents, it couldn't be used any other way except for in its printed or PDF format.

As a result, customers who needed to find information about their specific product—such as how to install a new battery—were forced to not just dig around the website to find their model's documentation, but also to then download the complete manual to access that tidbit of knowledge.

Today the company is investing in a better, more reusable way: a single repository of technical content written in chunks called "topics" and arranged using DITA, the XML schema designed for technical documentation we touched on in Chapter 6.

The approach is designed to give users access to technical documentation on demand—that is, just the topic module a customer needs, when he needs it, delivered online in a searchable format—while also streamlining the process for producing the printed pieces the company must ship with its products, all using the same reusable store of content.

You might think the hardest part of a project like this would be understanding DITA or doing the technical implementation, but that's often not the case. Many organizations that undertake a project like this find that it's actually most difficult to help the people involved change how they operate: the technical writers who are used to creating Word documents for their manuals, not crafting short little nuggets that answer a single question and saving them in a CMS module.

To cope with this challenge, enterprises that launch these sorts of content repositories need to invest in ongoing training and guidance—and also figure out where to start. For example, this company first focused on updating its print manual creation process to use the new structured, component-based system, because despite the importance of digital content, it still has to ship each product with printed materials for compliance reasons. By first training writers to craft DITA topic modules that culminate in printed documents, the project team was able to make writers feel more at home, increasing their confidence in the new method. From there, beginning to use the topic modules for other purposes was much easier.

Once you have a content repository in place for one purpose, you can also start looking at how you might be able to extend its value beyond a single application. For example, you might find that your customer service team also uses similar content for its own internal documentation. You could then hook their versions of the same content into the central system as well. That way, customer service can update the content with any customizations it needs, while still keeping all the content, in all its versions, in one centralized location, and eliminating the inefficiency of re-creating content.

Not ready for totally automating your content's publication across platforms? That doesn't mean a content store won't work for you. Done right, a content repository can manage multiple versions of the same content at any given time, each with different metadata associated with it. That way, different groups can repurpose different versions of the same basic chunk of content in many ways—some more manually, some more automatically.

As long as your content is structured based on its meaning and stored in a central place, you can build systems based on that structure to make finding and retrieving the content item you want to use simple and quick—and to ensure you're always starting from the latest, most updated source content, even if you're then going to manipulate it manually for certain circumstances.

## Content Across Products

The need for content that can cross devices and applications isn't limited to major media outlets like NPR, nor to enterprises publishing technical content. In fact, online retailers may be the ones who are most ahead of the game on delivering content—that is, their product information—from one database to many device-specific destinations.

Just look at Amazon.com, the online purveyor of books and, well, pretty much everything else. In addition to its desktop site, Amazon offers a wide range of mobile-optimized and device-specific products: a mobile site; shopping apps for iPhone, Android, BlackBerry, Windows 7, and iPad; barcode-scanning apps for iPhone and Android; a book-browsing app for iPad; and others with even more niche purposes.

What do all these distinct experiences have in common? Their content, of course. Using a private API, like those we talked about in Chapter 7, "Making Sense of Content APIs," Amazon can easily transport any or all of its millions of product listings it chooses—each full of descriptions, specs, images, reviews, and more structured content—to any or all of these apps and sites.

But Amazon doesn't use all product content in the same way across all these destinations. For example, the browsing iPad app, Windowshop, is designed for users who want to sit back and leaf through categories like bestsellers or baby gear. When you select a product, as I've done with Cheryl Strayed's book *Wild* in Figure 10.1, it puts visual content front and center, while tucking away descriptions and reviews in tabs along the left.

FIGURE 10.1
Windowshop for iPad, an app from Amazon designed around browsing books and other merchandise, prioritizes images over descriptions. Yet all of Amazon's digital products rely on the same set of content, reused across platforms via an API.

Meanwhile, PriceCheck, the iPhone barcode scanner, emphasizes much more straightforward content: the product's name and price, as shown in Figure 10.2. After all, if you've picked up a product and bothered to scan its barcode, odds are good you already know a bit about it and primarily want to assess whether you should buy it in store or order it. But if needed, additional content—including professional and customer reviews, ratings, publisher information, and more—are all tucked one swipe away.

FIGURE 10.2 PriceCheck, another app from Amazon—this one for iPhone. PriceCheck emphasizes content related specifically to purchasing products, but it still pulls from the same set of content as other Amazon experiences.

While Amazon's API has enabled the company to more easily share the same content base across products, it's not without its issues. For example, as Karen McGrane has noted, content often truncates on smaller screens, leaving off important parts of a book's title or cutting a review before it's communicated much of anything, like it does in Figure 10.3 with Amazon's own review of one of Dickens' well-known works.

FIGURE 10.3 "Bleak House is a satirical look at the byzantine legal system in England as it consumes the minds and talents of..." Damn. It was just getting good, wasn't it?

And that's the trouble: Only the first three lines of copy are displayed for each content element, regardless of what that element is—meaning that the most important information, such as the product description or features, has exactly the same amount of information revealed as the details about the publication date and publisher: around 120 characters. But the people producing that content weren't thinking about it displaying in such a short space, so their prose often takes that much space just to get warmed up. As a result, these content chunks often fail to provide anything useful, thus making the content difficult to do much with at a glance.

It would be easy to say that Amazon's problem is content reuse—that the company is causing usability and experience flaws by trying to force-fit the same content to all these different products. But I'd argue the real problem isn't that they're reusing content—no one's about to write custom content for each product for each of the millions of products Amazon sells, after all, so what other option is there? The underlying issue is structure: Amazon's content—structured as it is—isn't chunked in parts small enough to be exposed, layered, combined, or prioritized effectively on all those screen sizes.

While reusing content has allowed Amazon to quickly and efficiently build new digital products to meet user and business needs, the company could have made these experiences even stronger if it had considered what each piece of content was communicating, how the various chunks needed to work together, and how much of which sorts of content should be revealed when making decisions about the API's structure and substance, as we learned in Chapter 7. If it had, perhaps important content, like product names, would get a bit more room to breathe—and less important content, like publisher information, would get truncated.

And as we learned in Chapter 9, "Adaptable Content," if you're the one making these decisions, this is also the perfect time to take a step back and assess: Do you really need all this content in the first place? Could you tighten it up, cut some crap, and get to the good stuff more quickly—without sacrificing sales or frustrating customers? You'll never have a better opportunity to find out.

*The first information architect hired at Razorfish back in 1998, Karen McGrane
knows a thing or two million about organizing information in usable, useful ways—
and mobile is no exception. She's the author of* Content Strategy for Mobile *from A
Book Apart, a sought-after speaker, and one of the first people you should pay attention to if you care about content—for mobile or otherwise.*

### Why is developing a content strategy for mobile so important?

It's clear organizations are going to have to figure out how to structure and
distribute their content across a wide range of different platforms and systems—
smartphones and tablets, for sure, but as touchscreens get cheaper, hardware gets
smaller, and voice recognition gets more accurate, we're going to see a whole new
generation of devices on which our content will appear.

So why focus on mobile? Because right now, that's the buzzword on everyone's
lips. The CEO probably isn't kept up at night worrying how her content will appear
on a refrigerator touchscreen or in a voice-activated audio system in her car. But if
she's smart, she's worried about getting her content onto smartphones and tablets.

Fortunately, it's not an either/or proposition. Organizations that set themselves up
for success now on mobile will be well positioned to get their content onto other
new devices and platforms in the future. We need content strategy for mobile
because it's a catalyst that will help us make all our content better.

### What are some of the biggest challenges publishers face?

It's very easy to make the mistake of treating mobile like it's a completely separate
thing. Mobile sits in its own group in the org chart. Teams create a stand-alone app
or website that has different content. Updating the content requires a completely
separate workflow, and it's not hooked up to the CMS. They don't have a holistic way
to look at analytics data across all channels. That's short-term thinking.

Organizations need an overall content strategy that gives them an integrated
approach to their content, wherever it might appear. Remember: You don't get to
decide which device your customer uses to consume your content. Your customers decide that.

### Mobile can mean so many different things. How can organizations get started?

Mobile can be overwhelming. There are so many different options for how to approach it. Debates about which approach is best get heated—mobile Web versus native apps, responsive design versus separate templates—and people get religious.

That's actually why I guide people to think about their content and their publishing process before jumping into design and development approaches. By developing a content strategy for mobile, organizations are hopefully better positioned for the future, because they'll have more flexibility. The basic content strategy process offers a good guide for organizations as they move to multichannel publishing.

### How can we use mobile as a catalyst for better content across the board?

I don't advocate that organizations think about creating content uniquely for mobile. Who can afford to create content for just one channel? What I do advocate is that organizations use mobile as a lens to help them improve all their content. Here's a chance to inventory and audit your content and remove what doesn't deserve to be on mobile (which means it most likely shouldn't be on the desktop either). Here's a chance to edit your content to be more concise and written more clearly (that's not "writing for mobile," however—that's just good writing). Here's a chance to develop a more efficient workflow for publishing structured content and to develop a more usable content management system. Thinking about a content strategy for mobile isn't just about publishing content to smartphones or tablets—it's about using mobile as a catalyst within your organization to fix content and processes that just aren't working today. We might never see a better opportunity to fix what's broken, so let's use mobile to our advantage.

*Pick up* Content Strategy for Mobile, *and read more from McGrane at* karenmcgrane.com.

# Personalized Content

Content reuse isn't just about repurposing the same content to different platforms. It's also about repurposing and reorganizing it for different people, based on their personal requirements and desires.

This approach to personalized content, where a user can select the information she needs and create her own unique set of dashboards, reports, or other content collections, is becoming increasingly important in areas like healthcare, government, and education—places where users require different information depending on their needs, and where they tend to return regularly for news and updates.

As we touched on briefly in Chapter 7, the FCC launched just such a personalized content project in late 2011: my.fcc.gov. Unlike fcc.gov, which is geared toward consumers who have a problem that they need FCC information to solve, MyFCC is a beta site designed for frequent visitors, such as the telecommunications industry and the legal community that serves it, to create personal collections of FCC content.

This content—the same content that's available on the FCC's main site—is reused on MyFCC via the agency's API, and can be displayed in any order and priority the user chooses. For example, a telecoms attorney in the accessibility field may need to always stay abreast of the latest official documents and filings the FCC publishes about accessibility. With the MyFCC site, she can establish a dashboard that just includes those desired content modules, as shown in Figure 10.4, which are updated on the fly whenever new content arrives via the API.

While designed primarily for those users with frequent FCC business, everyone who wants to—from government officials down to interested citizens—can create and save their own MyFCC dashboards, dragging and dropping as many of the site's two dozen or so content widgets as they please wherever they want, and easily adding new ones or changing up the configuration anytime.

In addition to allowing users to create personalized content centers, this approach also lets the FCC's audiences take that content with them—that is, to mash up their MyFCC content with other organizations' information, and plug those modules into other sites as needed.

As we talked about in Chapter 7, when you open your content up by establishing an API, you can make this kind of reuse—across different sites, users, and needs—possible, efficiently. And, once you have an API in place that powers content personalization or reuse, you may well identify new purposes for that API in the future, giving your content even more places it can go.

FIGURE 10.4

A sample MyFCC dashboard, where a content API powers a personalized experience that allows you to quickly access just the reports,
news, and other content you want.

# A Reuse Imperative

If you think reuse is taking off now, just wait. Pretty soon, you'll see not
just the FCC, but all of the federal government's many entities get on the
bandwagon. That's right: What could be the largest content producer in the
United States is embracing reusable content.

Often seen as complex, bureaucratic, and slow moving, the U.S. government
is now actively changing how it operates by adopting more flexible, future-
ready strategies and technologies for content.

This shift has been underway for a while, and lots of agencies are already
experimenting with projects similar to the FCC's API. But the effort became
a coordinated, government-wide mandate in May 2012 with the White

House's release of "Digital Government: Building a 21st Century Platform to Better Serve the American People"—a new strategic initiative which includes, as one of its four main pillars, the goal of developing "an information-centric approach"—one that "moves us from managing 'documents' to managing discrete pieces of open data and content which can be tagged, shared, secured, mashed up and presented in the way that is most useful for the consumer of that information."[1]

Wowza. That's a lot to bite off—but it's exactly the sort of future-friendly approach we've been talking so much about, right?

In this new model, government is tasked with operating in a "customer-centric" way, rather than a bureaucratic, agency-oriented manner—meaning they'll not only be creating and sharing content using APIs, but they'll also be using and reusing that content in multiagency, multichannel ways, putting the experience of the customer who needs the content—you and I, that is—ahead of the specific agency that's producing it.

According to the report, this new approach to digital government also "influences how we create, manage, and present data through websites, mobile applications, raw data sets, and other modes of delivery, and allows customers to shape, share and consume information, whenever and however they want it"—in other words, providing personalized content, structured and organized in whatever way a user needs.

Why's this initiative such a big deal? Well, if you think you've got problems with duplicative, redundant, or hard-to-sort content, just imagine what the U.S. government is dealing with: 450 million pages of digital content, according to Todd Parks, a longtime Silicon Valley entrepreneur who joined the Obama administration in 2009 and became the CTO of the United States in 2012.[2]

For example, when the digital government initiative launched, Parks noted that the government was running 14 separate websites for students seeking information about federal financial aid—one for applying, one for managing loans, one for consolidating student loans, and so on—each operating independently, and each producing its own content (just a few of those sites are shown here in Figures 10.5–10.7).

---

1 Read the whole report at http://rfld.me/QjTUpd.

2 You can watch the entire video of Parks and U.S. CIO Steven Van Roeckel launching the initiative at Techcrunch Disrupt on May 23, 2012, here: http://rfld.me/Olewe3.

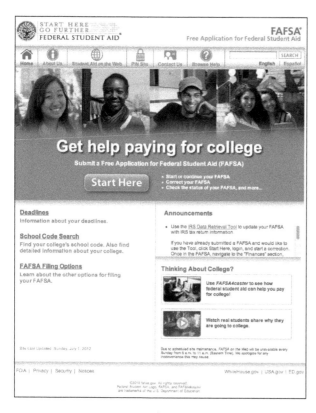

FIGURE 10.5
The Free Application for Federal Student Aid site, fafsa.ed.gov, one of more than a dozen websites related to federal student aid.

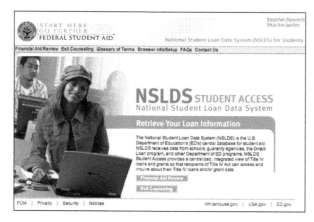

FIGURE 10.6
Another of the federal government's student aid sites, the National Student Loan Data System at nslds.ed.gov. Here borrowers can manage their federal loans.

FIGURE 10.7
And yet another
separate federal
student aid site,
loanconsolidation.
ed.gov, where those
same borrowers must
go to find out how
to consolidate their
student loans.

What the government realized is that all these siloed sites with variations on the same information were taking lots of time and money to manage—time and money that wasn't actually serving the government's customer: the constituents who need to get things done, and don't care whether they're supposed to visit the NSLDS or the FAFSA (or the Small Business Association or the Federal Trade Commission, for that matter) to do it.

As part of the solution, the initiative effectively bans establishing new .gov domains—so the days of building a website for every new initiative are effectively over. But the broader goal is so much bigger: To end this era of thousands of government websites and millions of pages of locked-down, hard-to-find content, and replace it with one built on open data, machine-readable content, and APIs that transmit information wherever it needs to go.

What will it take? Well, transforming government is no small task. A huge number of those 450 million pages of content are locked into fixed, hard-to-adapt documents like PDFs. To get there, the government is pulling content out of fixed objects like these, and into clean databases that are separated from their display, readying them for both public and private APIs.

What'll happen with all this data? Take an example like flu.gov, shown in Figure 10.8—a federal site run by the Department of Health & Human Services to help the public prevent, prepare for, identify, and treat the flu.

While flu.gov seeks to be *the* resource for Americans who need flu information, "Flu" isn't the name of a government agency, of course. Instead, it's a site that uses content and data from myriad government agencies: the Centers for Disease Control, the National Institutes of Health, and the Federal Drug Administration, just to name a few.

FIGURE 10.8

Flu.gov, which reuses content from across multiple agencies like the CDC, NIH, and FDA to create a user-centered, useful site for the American people—instead of for a specific agency.

Each of these agencies is tasked with performing different research and producing its own specific reports, but none of that matters much to the American people, who just want to find accurate, up-to-date information about the flu and any current outbreaks, affected communities, symptoms, and treatment methods.

What better way to present all that flu-related content than to collect it in one place, rather than expect the public to find it when scattered across multiple sites? And that's exactly what the government is working toward, with some content—including that of the CDC, for example—already being accessed via API and reused by flu.gov automatically, and more to come as the digital government initiative grows.

## And Now for Something Completely Different

Serving up different content combinations across different platforms or to different users is relatively easy when you have a well-structured database and content-focused API behind you. But what if you're trying to reuse content that wasn't created under such ideal terms? What can you do with content that's deeply rooted in a print production process, besides start over from scratch?

Where there's a will, there's a way. Just as many organizations are experimenting with ways to get more mileage out of each piece of digital content they produce, others are also doing interesting things in order to make the most of print material—and their existing print production practices.

Take the *Guardian*, a major daily newspaper with a large online presence in the UK. In publication for nearly two centuries, the *Guardian* has spent its recent years embracing social media and mobile wholeheartedly, launching apps and sites for everything from iOS and Android to Kindle, Nokia, and even Facebook.

In 2011, the *Guardian* decided to try something different than the standard mobile fare of up-to-the-minute news stories: It launched a tablet edition of the daily paper. Unlike its other digital products, which provide readers with an ever-changing experience, the design team built this particular product to deliver "a reflective once-a-day Guardian, designed and edited for iPad," noted editor-in-chief Alan Rusbridger shortly after the app's launch. By following the concept of the *Guardian*'s print edition, the organization sought to bring those readers who enjoy the daily snapshot of news the print edition provides with a way to have that experience in a digital format.

But putting the paper online as a PDF wouldn't cut it design- or usability-wise, and the *Guardian,* like all papers, has to continually operate under tight deadlines to get the next day's edition out the door and ready for readers. So how was the organization going to deliver a tablet edition without hiring a bunch of extra hands to import the stories and design each day's iPad layout from scratch?

Rather than running their designers ragged by essentially creating a PDF-like version of the print newspaper specifically for iPad (or worse yet, creating two PDFs—one in portrait and the other in landscape), the team opted for something a bit more content-focused and a lot less time-consuming to perform on a daily basis. It decided to start analyzing its print content's structure in order to re-create that same sense of priority, hierarchy, and importance on the iPad—while simultaneously taking advantage of the new form factor and functionality. You can see the result in Figure 10.9.

FIGURE 10.9
Rather than dismantling its daily paper production process, the *Guardian* takes its print edition and mechanically analyzes the way stories are prioritized; it then uses business rules to keep those same relationships in place for this daily iPad edition.

How does it work? Well, the *Guardian* team built a script that can (nearly) automatically read the InDesign files for the print version of the paper, assess them according to predetermined criteria—such as page number, amount of space devoted to the story, positioning on the page, headline and image sizing, and the like—and then assign them a score. That value is then carried into a new InDesign template for the app, and the stories are rebuilt automatically based on their score. Effectively, this means that the editorial eye and manual art direction that went into the print edition are automatically taken into account for the iPad version, rather than investing that same level of human care all over again for the new platform.

The automation isn't perfect, but it gives the *Guardian* a solid first draft. From there, editors and designers can easily go through the iPad edition each night, ensuring everything's as it should be and making tweaks to keep the experience polished and usable. But, in comparison to crafting the iPad edition from scratch, this manual investment is miniscule.

## Chasing Perfection

Once you start working with reusable content, it's easy to start obsessing over a dream: a world where all content can be perfectly reused everywhere you need it, and where content production becomes as set-it-and-forget-it as a Ronco Rotisserie Oven.

Alas, that's not to be. Content is work. Content takes people. And content certainly doesn't do well when it's treated like a factory-produced commodity (see also: content farms, SEO spammers, and low-rent link aggregators). While reusing and establishing systems for centralized content stores can be incredibly effective, nothing good will come from getting obsessed over it working perfectly, without human intervention, for every single output in the world.

Instead, relax. Making your content more reusable isn't about mechanizing your entire process. While some reuse evangelists might make it seem otherwise, there are likely plenty of good reasons to handcraft some of your content—to carefully, manually, painstakingly make your content sing for one specific output, rather than pull from a generic listing.

Sometimes.

Fact is, you have to make choices: choices about what's important enough to invest your limited time and budget and sleepless nights on, and what isn't. And those choices come down to understanding what you're trying to accomplish and whether repurposing content will help you do it or not.

Of course, even if you choose to handcraft quite a lot of your content, there's still something to be said for building a central content repository or asset library—one place from which all critical content assets can be managed and maintained, updated and archived—and using it as your source content. Because from there, whoever is responsible for crafting custom content for a specific purpose or destination can be confident he's working from the latest and greatest source material—without spending endless time hunting down information or asking people in multiple departments to provide material.

## Making Reuse Meaningful

Whether your organization wants to allow customers to develop their own personalized collections of content, provide internal teams with access to up-to-date source material, automate publishing across multiple platforms and devices, or even try something more experimental, structured content will help you get there—gracefully.

By breaking your content down along the lines that matter, you've done what it takes to make your content ready for reuse—and, just as critically, to know whether or not it makes sense for reuse in the first place.

Now that we've covered content that's reusable and reconfigurable across all the systems and channels under your purview, it's time for something weirder—how content travels outside your control. In Chapter 11, "Transportable Content," we'll tackle content that goes beyond your bounds, transported by your users to places you may not even be able to imagine yet.

CHAPTER 11

Transportable Content

The Great Content Shift                            175
What's in It for You?                              178
Taking Advantage of Content Shifting              179
More Portability, More Problems                   182
What You Can Do                                   185
Letting Go                                        186

We've talked a lot about what *you* can do with structured, smart, reusable content. But guess what? You're not the only one who'll want to shovel it around the Internet. Your users likely will, too, shifting your content from wherever you put it into their own preferred destinations for reading, sharing, and using it.

You can already see this in action with hugely popular services like Pinterest, where users install a bookmarklet in their browser and "pin" images and video they like to "boards" of their own—creating collections of content around topics like vacation ideas or interior design inspiration. It's also the crux of read-later apps like Safari's Reader, Readability, Instapaper, and Pocket (formerly called Read it Later), which at a quick click or tap take content from its source and pull it into a user's own collection on that service's servers, allowing her to read it later in a clean, clutter-free interface (as shown with an example from Salon.com, then displayed in Readability, in Figures 11.1 and 11.2).

It's even cropping up in more niche services like Gimme Bar—where users can collect not just images and video like in Pinterest, but also complete screen shots, text snippets, audio, and other content—and Svpply, which allows users to create collections of products they want, browse and mark the collections of others as favorites, and click through any product to shop on a retailer's website.

FIGURE 11.1
An article about the acclaimed TV show *Breaking Bad* on salon.com, where it's surrounded by plenty of distraction.

FIGURE 11.2
The start of that same article pulled into Readability, where the content now runs the show.

Each of these examples offers users a different design and features, but they all come back to the same central theme: giving users the power to pluck a piece of content from its original location and shift it to another context. Unlike bookmarking the page, which just creates a link to the content, these services are actually helping users put that content in their digital pocket, so to speak, and carry it around with them.

> **NOTE** WHAT IS CONTENT SHIFTING?
>
> *Content shifting*, as I use it in this chapter, is the process of taking content from one context—as in, a specific website or application—and shifting it to another location. People shift content for a wide range of reasons. They may want a cleaner interface for reading, seek to save the content for later, include the content in a collection of similar pieces, or need to access it at a time when they won't have an Internet connection. Whatever the reason, though, people are shifting content more and more often—and tools are cropping up left and right to help them do it.

In this chapter, we'll talk about how content is becoming more transportable—oftentimes, whether you want it to or not—as well as the opportunities, challenges, and ethical considerations at play for those creating, managing, and organizing that content. Finally, we'll explore where this emerging trend may go in the future, and what you can do to not just deal with it, but help shape it.

## The Great Content Shift

> Our transformed relationship with content is one in which individual users are the gravitational center and content floats in orbit around them.
>
> —Cameron Koczon[1]

A few different terms have cropped up for this new form of content transportation and consumption, including time-shifted content, portable content, and orbital content, as Koczon—part of Fictive Kin, the startup behind Gimme Bar—coined it. Whatever you call it, all these phrases point to the same reality: While users may want your content (and if they don't, you should stop right now and go fix *that* problem first), they don't necessarily want to get it on your website.

---

1  If you haven't yet, do read Koczon's whole article from *A List Apart:* http://rfld.me/MhSwou.

Instead, they want it in the place that's most comfortable for them, and from which they can easily share it and save it for later. They also want to turn pieces of content from lots of different sources into their personal collection—not a list of bookmarks, but a compilation of the content itself.

This presents a big mental shift for many of us. After all, we're used to the model we made two decades ago—a model where people "surf" (or, since it's not the '90s anymore, "browse"), find your stuff, and come back to it whenever they want to see it again.

It's not that this behavior no longer exists. For the foreseeable future at least, plenty of folks will still type in your URL or add your site to their favorites menu. The difference is that now, that's just one way information will be consumed.

It's hard to pinpoint a single reason for this shift, but I'd argue it's got a lot to do with the amount of content each of us is coming in contact with online. Tweets and news articles and blogs and products seem to pop onto the collective radar incredibly quickly, and to whiz by faster than anyone can reasonably keep up with. In all likelihood, your users are feeling overwhelmed, and they're looking for a way to keep up with the flow and make sense of the things that are important to them. These services can help them easily save the interesting bits that would otherwise flit by, avoiding the painful experience of trying to recollect who shared which link and then searching through pages of updates to find it again.

But that's not all. This shift also seems like a clear response to the problems with the online reading experience. As we touched on in Chapter 10, "Reusable Content," sitting down with a long read online often results in a frustratingly distracting experience—one where the actual content receives so little page real estate, it's hard to even tell what you're looking at. Standing in stark contrast to print design, where pages are often lovingly laid out once content and imagery are complete—beautifully showcasing typography, photography, and design elements that contribute to the story—online versions often weigh readers down with a metric ton of advertising, all of it seemingly blinking and expanding and taking over the screen until you can barely see straight.

Take the example from SFGate shown in Figure 11.3, where I'm hit with multiple banner ads, two types of advertising for other products from the *Chronicle*, and even an annoying ad for art print retailer 20x200, "retargeted" to me because I've visited the retailer's site before.

Now, SFGate relies on that advertising to support its business model, so perhaps you could argue it has an excuse for creating such a cluttered reading experience. But what about sites that don't rely on advertising revenue? Many of them are still cluttering up their content with endless noisy distractions, like the GoDaddy hosting page shown in Figure 11.4, which seems to desperately want you to buy something (though with all the clutter, I have a rather hard time figuring out what).

**FIGURE 11.3**

Noise, noise, noise: three banners, one expandable ad overlay, and two ads for the *Chronicle*'s other products take over the first few hundred pixels of SFGate.com.

**FIGURE 11.4**

Yet another reason to never use GoDaddy: overwhelming, cluttered, and way-too-pushy pages that make it nearly impossible to know where to go and what's important.

In the face of the myriad less-than-reader-friendly experiences users face every day, is it any surprise many would rather skip your site altogether and transfer the content they want to a place that's been designed around...you know...*reading*?

Finally, people are still human when they go online. And humans want to connect with others, share the things that matter to them, and be social. As more and more communication takes place online, it's no surprise people want to use digital platforms to share content and show one another the things they've been collecting, coveting, and reading as well. The digital possibilities may be new, but the desire to share and compare is anything but.

## What's in It for You?

So we can see why a user might want to save, shift, and share your content. But why should you embrace this movement, too? What's in it for content creators and publishers—and those who help them plan and organize online experiences—anyway?

For one, it's a matter of making your content easier for new audiences to discover it and share it with others, as Svpply does very well. With this service, users create collections of products they want. Others can "Want" that product, too, with an action not unlike the Facebook Like button, as shown in Figure 11.5.

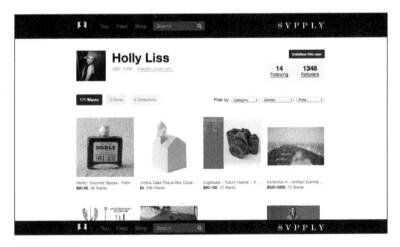

FIGURE 11.5
Svpply's approach: Let users pluck products they love, create personal collections, and share them with one another. From here, it's easy to click through to buy the product directly from the seller.

If you're a retailer, there's nothing better than other people putting your content front and center for their friends and followers to see it, click on it, and—you hope—buy it.

While this sort of content collection is a no-brainer for ecommerce, the benefit of greater content syndication extends beyond products. In any industry, if you have content that helps people solve a problem or complete a task—while also remaining somehow relevant to whatever your products or services actually are—then you'd benefit from getting more people to know about that content.

It's not all about increasing your reach, though. Another big—and often ignored—benefit to embracing content shifting and sharing services is that you're building deeper connections between your users and your brand. Think about it this way: when users pocket your content for their personal collection, they're essentially saying that your stuff is worth keeping. They're not taking content away from you; they're taking a piece of you along with them. And that's a powerful thing.

## Taking Advantage of Content Shifting

As you've probably already guessed (this book has a theme, after all), one of the biggest ways you can make your content work better wherever it's being viewed is by giving it structure. Why? Because when your content has structure that's machine-readable and ready to be parsed, it's much easier for those content-shifting services to keep the intent of your content intact, retaining elements like bylines and datelines, displaying copy decks in distinctive large type, and generally leaving you with a layout that still communicates what you intended.

But if you've used things like font size and bolding to differentiate parts of content, those services will have a much more difficult time knowing what to do with them—and that makes for content that causes some problems when it gets shifted. For example, take a look at an article from Columbia University's news section, shown in Figure 11.6, and that same article displayed with Instapaper in Figure 11.7.

"That's OK," you might say. "At least it looks good on our site." But you know who suffers when your content parses poorly? Your users—the people who liked your content or product enough to share it and save it for later.

FIGURE 11.6

An article from Columbia University's news section, featuring a video and Q&A with a professor.

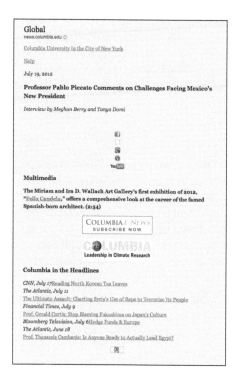

FIGURE 11.7

That same article displayed via Instapaper—except all the content's missing! While scrapping the video was expected, what happened to the Q&A? All that's left is some out-of-context "related content" and social links from the sidebar.

Instapaper actually already offers publishers guidelines for making their content ready for parsing, providing specific tags that make it easy for Instapaper to understand the content's title, date, author, and body, and also to ensure all parts of multipage pieces are pulled in.[2] This is a good start, because it gets everyone thinking about content chunks.

The problem is, it's too specific to one output (Instapaper) and to one type of content (articles). If you want to prepare your content for a future that's all about unknowns, you can't rely on marking it up for individual destinations. If you do, you'll end up with a mess of code that must be updated each time a new service is unveiled.

The good news is, by applying the skills learned throughout this book—breaking content down, storing it in modular parts, and using metadata and markup to keep its meaning intact—you can keep your content making sense for your users, even when it's shifted.

---

2  See Instapaper's publisher tools at http://rfld.me/PkjiXJ.

Plus, when it comes to content shifting, we're just getting started. As we'll talk about next, there's lots to work out when it comes to issues like attribution, circulation, and compensation. Which means if you have content structured according to its meaning and stored with solid metadata now, you'll be ahead of the game as new standards emerge for marking up content for shifting contexts.

# More Portability, More Problems

Content shifting is fascinating, but it's not a simple topic. The idea of users plucking your content from one location and consuming, sharing, and saving it somewhere else can be scary, especially if you're working with a site that relies on advertising to support its business model. Just like television executives got wide-eyed and terrified when they first saw TiVo—"What'll we do if everyone just speeds past the commercials?"—today, publishers and their legal counsels have plenty of reasons to fear content that's been shifted away from its original context.

When you look carefully, this fear of content-shifting, saving, and clutter-removing apps is actually about more than money (though that's certainly a large part of it). It's about three closely interrelated issues: attribution, copyright, and compensation.

Let's look quickly at each problem and some solutions.

## Attribution

Take a spin through Pinterest, and you'll find thousands of beautiful images: high-fashion photography that looks like it could be straight from the pages of *Vogue*; gorgeous architectural shots that would make any designer drool; stunning landscapes and exotic travel destinations, like those shown in Figure 11.8. But where do they all come from?

Sure, you can tell what site they were pinned from, and get a link back to that page. But there's no actual attribution to be found—and no metadata that comes along with each image. Instead, when a user plucks a picture and pins it, as of this writing, Pinterest hosts that image on its servers, stripping away any descriptive content that was once with it.

When content-shifting and sharing services pull content from one location and place it in another without including any attribution, it's no surprise that those creating content—such as professional photographers—might get a little antsy. At the same time, this problem isn't new. Whether you look back a couple years to Tumblr's rise or a couple decades to the mixtape, people have been plucking content from one place and saving their own versions of it for quite some time. It's simply now much easier to do—and, perhaps more important, easier to see just how many people are doing it.

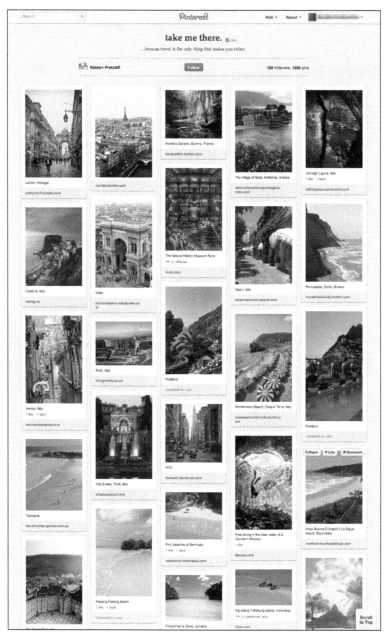

FIGURE 11.8

A typical Pinterest board, featuring photos collected from across the Web and arranged in the site's signature minimal style. But where do these images come from, and who owns them? It's hard to say.

## Copyright

When you shift content from its original location to your preferred destination—whether you're saving it to your desktop, pasting it into a Word document, or using one of the services we've talked about in this chapter—you're copying it, plain and simple. And when you start talking about copying, you pretty much can't avoid talking about copyright.

While attribution deals with keeping track of where content is from and who created it, copyright is about something subtly different: whether or not someone else has the right to reproduce the work. But reproduction alone doesn't constitute a copyright violation. Many of these services consider what they do to be fair use—that is, a legal reproduction of copyrighted material that doesn't require permission—because they're enabling users to save content for personal use, rather than copying it for their own distribution.

Thing is, copyright is a tricky subject in the United States, where most of these services are centered, because it's decided on a case-by-case basis—and while there are fair use guidelines, they're all relative and open for a judge's interpretation: how much of the original work is being reproduced; whether the content's meaning is transformed in the process; whether the reproduction affects the value of the original; what sort of entity is reproducing the work; etc.

With so many factors involved, it would be hard to say exactly where each service falls in legal terms without a few expensive, soul-crushing court battles taking place. But what is clear is that many content creators aren't happy with the way their copyrighted materials are being used—and some, particularly those that are well organized and can afford the legal fees, are likely to push the copyright issue front and center soon.

## Compensation

This, of course, is the kicker for so many content creators. Lots of people make money off digital content, typically via advertising revenue. So it's no surprise that when users shift that content and strip the ads away, those who build their business on advertising get a bit upset.

Readability tried an experimental approach to solving this business-model problem: actually paying the publishers whose content was shifted using Readability. For about a year, Readability's publisher payment program accepted subscription fees from users, typically $5 a month, and set aside that money to pay the publishers whose content was being consumed via Readability's products. By tracking how often a given publisher's work was read using the service, Readability hoped to distribute the money it received fairly, and in the process, to make progress toward a new model for paid content.

But Readability discontinued the program in the spring of 2012 because too few publishers participated, and most of the funds earmarked for publisher payments had gone unclaimed. With more than $150,000 in a bank account meant to pay content creators and producers, Readability disbanded the program and donated the bulk of its coffers to charity.

Of course, Readability isn't the only organization trying to come up with alternatives to the advertising business model. But despite all the Kickstarters and other services out there, it's clear no one has a workable answer to the compensation question yet—and most publishers, already obsessed with pageviews and continually adding clutter to their sites, are struggling to do much besides get riled up and angry.

Attribution, copyright, and compensation are weighty issues, to be sure—issues I'm pretty hesitant to predict the precise future of. But all said, it's easy to paint those presenting us with new content-shifting services as the bad guys: malicious startups trying to make a splash by further eroding online media's already crumbling business model. But I'd argue that's too easy—and, moreover, that those of us who work with content are a part of the problem, because we've failed to rethink what our content means in an online, unbounded world.

Those who are experimenting, building things like Safari Reader, Instapaper, or Pinterest? While their own business models may not be figured out yet either, and while their ability to parse content's meaning and support it with solid attribution may still need work, they're taking necessary first steps toward finding a model that makes sense in a digital world.

Are you going to take steps, too?

## What You Can Do

So readers are frustrated, people like to share, applications are experimenting, content publishers are crying foul, and business models are collapsing. Amid the hubbub, what should you actually *do* about it?

Many organizations are reacting by trying to rein in content that's being shifted and shared, preventing people from saving it for later, sharing it with their friends, or shifting it to a more reader-friendly layout. And it's perfectly understandable why. If these new technologies and services allow a user to strip away everything she doesn't want and just take the content that matters to her, then what loyalty does that user have to the place she got the content? Will she even know where it's from? Will she care?

We don't have all the answers, but I'd argue your best course of action is to think of the people who want your content in their collection as allies waiting to happen. They care about you. They think you're great. So you can alienate them by being stingy, or you can turn this into an opportunity for you—by being an active part of this shift, rather than someone this shift *happens to*. Here's how.

### Be Part of the Experiment

Experimentation isn't just for startups. In every field, we need folks willing to experiment with new ways to publish, share, pay for, and circulate content. After all, it's beyond obvious that the old pay-per-eyeball thing isn't working, and that too often, it's the content creators who are left in the lurch, paid peanuts for what's often thoughtful, researched, complex work.

If you care about solving the problem, then your first step is to get comfortable experimenting, too—to accept that this isn't all figured out yet, and to be willing to do things differently and see what happens. From launching Kickstarter campaigns to fund content projects to publishing a long article as a Kindle Single—a short ebook that Amazon sells for just a few dollars—there are lots of avenues to explore once you stop clinging to the old model. That doesn't mean any of them are perfect, but they're a place to start. And they won't get better unless we work on them.

### Improve the Reading Experience

Lots of times, you hear publishers and retailers say they want to design experiences that are "sticky"—that users will stay with for a long period of time and come back to frequently. One way to do that is to focus in on creating a great reading experience—one where the content takes center stage, and where visual cues help the reader focus and immerse, rather than become overwhelmed and distracted. After all, what better way to keep people from shifting your content to a reading service than to make your own site a comfortable place to read?

It might not be realistic to strip away every bit of supplementary content or call to action or advertising from your site, but it's worthwhile to take a hard look at all the stuff you're publishing and ask whether it really matters. If it doesn't, it's time to cut the cruft—before your users cut your site.

## Letting Go

We don't know what will happen as more people start to experiment. Services will launch and die out; innovation will be frequent, but disjointed.

Yet we do know this: When we stop wasting our time thinking about the "pages" where our content "lives," we can start thinking about all kinds of new opportunities and ideas. We can come up with new ways to create and distribute packages of information that work together—and travel together.

We can discuss new ways to track content circulation, embedding information in our content about where it's been and how often it's been used. We can experiment with new business models using the expertise of people on both sides of the equation: those who create great content, and those who appreciate it.

The point is, none of these problems has been solved just yet, and you won't have all the answers anytime soon. But if you want to be part of the group dedicated to figuring it out—and benefiting from the result—then you've got to let go: of outdated ideas about location and ownership; of concern for controlling every bit of your users' experience; of fear about where your content might end up. Because until you learn to let go of the past, you can't embrace—and be part of building—whatever's next.

Of course, it's not just that issues like attribution—or, for businesses that use content to gain loyalty and sell product, losing brand voice and messaging—aren't valid. Having your content lose its provenance is a very real concern, and one that only gets more important as content gets further away from the people making it.

But the truth is, there isn't any other option—not really. Your users aren't going to stop expecting to collect content and tote it around with them, and your organization is going to have a hell of a time trying to nail it all down.

Instead, letting go is all about committing to two things. First, you must accept that your content will be shifted and moved. You can find flaws in the business models of today's content-shifting services (and they do have many, no doubt). You can be wary of those who want a piece of your content, yet seem unencumbered by morals.

But the content itself? It's going to move beyond your control.

Second, you need to invest in content that's worth remembering—not necessarily for where it was found, but for what it meant and how it communicated that meaning. Great content is memorable, and being memorable is about more than your URL. It's about your voice, your message, and your ability to help others.

When your content does that, when your audience finds it and feels like it's intrinsically you—it's so much yours that it couldn't possibly be anyone else's—then in some ways, it matters much less where they found it.

But accepting that you can't control your content is going to take more than some structure and metadata, especially in an organization that's still thinking about controlling its message and maintaining the perfect PR spin. If your organization is obsessed with broadcasting its message—rather than allowing customers to define their own experiences—then you're only going to get more uncomfortable as the future unfolds.

So now that we've looked at myriad ways that your content, once it's structured and self-descriptive, might be adapted, reused, reprioritized, connected, dissected, and transported to meet the needs of a changing Web, it's time we take things one more step. In addition to changing our content, it's time we look at how to change our organizations themselves, and shift the role of content in the enterprises we work in or support. To do so, we'll now explore how organization-centric thinking harms organizations, creating lots of noise but leaving the signal to wither—and what you can do to stop it.

# PART IV

# Enduring Content

If we want content to endure—to live beyond a single use in a single place—then we have two demons to fight: the organizations, old-fashioned and behemoth, that keep people and ideas siloed; and the content itself, which can so easily lose its liveliness, beauty, art, and value as it's automatically reproduced. In this final section, you'll learn skills and approaches for dealing with both—resulting in content that endures, its purpose clear, its heart intact, whatever the future holds.

CHAPTER 12

# Content and Change

Why You? Why Now?                                192
Rethinking Content, Revealing Fracture          193
Making Change Stick                              194
Building a Team                                  198
Being on the Outside                             199
Dealing with Fear                               200
Putting People First                           200

Content is powerful. Done right, it can be useful, lovable, and memorable—even when it's being repurposed, reused, and reconfigured in countless ways. It can communicate critical information, share stories, and build connections. It can drive sales and increase customer satisfaction.

But it can also be powerful in a way you might not have yet considered: At its best, content can change organizations.

If you want to break content free from pages and documents and accept that your users will share and shift it in ways you can't control, you must also break it free from the organizational silos and roadblocks that put it in those fixed, inflexible formats in the first place: closed-off departments; top-down, anti-collaborative thinking; and me-first mentalities. Because you can't rally your entire organization around efficient, multichannel, reusable content if each department is still operating like it's everyone for herself. You'll always be stuck.

Being stuck is only getting more and more dangerous. The more rapidly the world embraces new platforms and your audiences embrace new communication tools, the less your organization can afford to cling to the past or stay in its comfort zone. You need to get nimble if you want to keep up.

That is, shifting for mobile is great. But it's only enough to get by *right now*. For a more sustainable future—one where you can embrace, not fear, the many ways your audiences want to consume your content—your organization needs to not just *change*. It needs to become an organization that is *adept at change*—and can do it time and time again.

## Why You? Why Now?

That's where you come in. When you work in IA, UX, and content strategy, it's easy to stay mired in the details, thinking about individual interaction problems or teasing out ways to improve individual processes. But because you've taken time to unravel your snarled ball of content and start thinking about its structure, relationships, and future, you're poised to turn that work into something greater.

How much time have you already invested in making your content more future-ready and flexible? How much more will it take once you're done reading this book? The fact is, if you want all that time to be truly worth it, you have to be willing to get out of the details and into making broad, far-reaching change—to get your organization to think and act differently.

If you don't focus your energy toward change, even the best-planned publishing program and perfectly structured CMS won't fix your problems. Marketing will still think its content is the only stuff that counts; the PR department will still insist on publishing endless PDFs of the same old press releases no one reads; and the IT team will still dictate tools that don't make sense for the skill sets and priorities of the people who'll be using them. And your users? Well, they couldn't care less about any of that. They simply want the information they need in a format that works for them.

For your content to go everywhere your customers demand, you must become a *linchpin,* as Seth Godin calls them: a person dedicated to change who can help your organization pivot and embrace practices that are truly customer focused, human, and sustainable. You have to begin to change the course of business as usual.

So how can you—as a content strategist, information architect, UX consultant, writer, editor, or whatever role you're playing—help make this happen? How should you fight for lively, lovable, usable content that crosses not just devices and channels, but departments and politics-as-usual as well?

In this chapter, we'll explore ways to get started.

# Rethinking Content, Revealing Fracture

We've all heard a lot the past few years about honesty and transparency in business—about human-centered, customer-focused products and practices. And yet, so many organizations simply hire a social media manager to communicate directly with customers on Twitter and call it a day.

That doesn't cut it.

Being human in business is about much more than replying to fans' comments. It's about making every aspect of how you operate focused on helping your customers or users get things done and live better lives. If that's not at the core, there's no social media campaign that can make your organization human, believable, or—perhaps most important—capable of adapting and shifting.

Take, for example, the U.S. government and its digital initiatives, which we explored in Chapter 10, "Reusable Content." One of the strongest forces behind its push for more API-driven, cross-department, cross-device digital content was to simply make government accessible—in other words, to publish content in the name of the people, not the name of the agency that happens to produce it, as the Digital Government report explains:

> The Federal Government needs to change to a culture of customer service. A key part of that shift is the need to start absorbing the complexity of the Government on behalf of the citizen. As one participant wrote, "Customers don't know—and don't care to know—how government is organized. So why make them go from agency [website] to agency [website] to get the full picture of what gov't has to offer on any subject?"[1]

It's too soon to tell how well the U.S. government can pull this off—and how their efforts will fare as the political winds shift and the powers that be change. It's got a lot of years of bureaucracy holding it back, after all. But the spirit of the initiative and the focus on achievable milestones guided by a central, multidisciplined team? Those are right on track.

As the federal government is learning, you can't get ready for the future while you operate the same as you always have. You have to start thinking across divides, be they organizational, departmental, functional, or political. And if you aren't, it'll show: content will stay siloed in a single website. Responsive designs will remain skin deep. Different groups will publish nearly the same content, each working independently—and wasting countless hours doing so. Users will continue to have trouble finding information, or reach dead ends rather than connections for further reading.

## Making Change Stick

If you've read this far, chances are you're ready to make change—that you're willing to do things differently, even when it seems difficult at first. After all, taking unstructured content, breaking it down, and building structures that will let it go further isn't exactly a relaxing weekend by the beach. Now, you also need to lend that spirit toward driving change in your organization, or convincing your client that change is worth working toward.

What does it actually take to make this flexible, adaptable approach to content an organizational reality—one that can be supported and sustained over time? What are the traits you should be looking for and encouraging others to value?

The larger and more complicated your organization is, the more effort will be required—because the more people you'll need to coordinate with, and the more kinks you'll need to work out. But no matter the size of your organization or the time it will take to get there, at the most basic level, you need three ingredients: clear vision, customer focus, and collaboration.

---

1   From the Digital Government report, available at http://rfld.me/QjTUpd. This particular gem is from Part C, on customer-centric thinking.

## Clear Vision

What's your organization's or your client's vision? Do you know? If the official answer starts with "to be the premier firm in...," then there's a problem—namely, you haven't actually got one.

When you have vision, you have a reason for existing—a reason that transcends revenue streams and, typically, specific products or services. It's a vision built on the role you'll play in your customers' or users' lives.

How do you know when vision is lacking? Once you start looking, it's actually pretty easy to spot: emphasis on the "bottom line" rather than on product or service quality, endlessly chasing after new clients or markets, departmental infighting over budgets and priorities, and disagreement over who your audience is—or the desire to have "everyone" as a customer.

All these things indicate a major problem: that no one has a clear idea of what's important—which clients or customers to go after, which products or services to build next, which information needs to be communicated most. Every initiative turns into a short-term game in the name of revenue rather than sustainability.

Without vision, you'll find it's impossible to get individual departments to work together—because if they don't know where the organization is headed, why should they invest in collaborating to help it get there? You'll also have a hell of a time making decisions about where you should be publishing and which channels are worth extra manual care, versus which should be handled in as automated a way as possible. When you don't know where you're going, it's pretty impossible to tell what's going to help you get there.

But take heart. Even if your organization's vision needs some help, it may not be in dire straits. It might just need a hearty shove in the right direction—and there might be no better shove than showing your management team how locked up, inaccessible, and useless their content is on mobile devices.

Yet vision can't be built on fear alone. While stats about mobile proliferation and the percentage of users visiting your content from non-desktop machines can be telling, your conversation can't end with your CEO in a panic attack.

That's where this book can help. Not only do you know how to start preparing your content and the things you should consider, but you also have a variety of examples to share with your team—like NPR's COPE model, the federal government's API-driven initiatives, or the BBC's incredible SEO results.

## Customer Focus

We've talked more about content than customers in this book, but don't let that mislead you. Preparing your content to go everywhere is actually, more than anything, about caring for your users—because it's all about getting your content onto all the platforms and places they want it.

Whether you're thinking about adapting for mobile, allowing users to create personal collections of content, improving their ability to find information, or any of the other things we've discussed in this book, the only reason to do any of it is to be where your customers are, rather than expecting them to always come to you. Like we talked about in Chapter 11, "Transportable Content," we're quickly approaching a time when users expect to be at the center, with collections of content that orbit them—rather than them orbiting around your organization's content.

When you're customer focused at the core of your organization, the prospect of allowing your content to go wherever your users take it stops seeming outlandish and starts seemingly like the only sensible course of action.

In other words, when you're truly thinking about your customer, you don't care about the device or platform. You don't want to put all your eggs in the desktop basket—or the iPhone app basket, for that matter. Instead, you put your business where your customers are—which must necessarily transcend all that.

So how can you tell if your organization is struggling with customer centricity? There are a few telltale signs that it's slipping away. One big one is if folks insist on asking new customers for excessive personal data because the "organization needs it." Others are defaulting opt-in checkboxes on a sign-up form to pre-selected, forcing your users to remember to opt out if they don't want to get spammed, or organizing a website around your internal organizational structure, rather than around your users' needs and mental model.

Another example of organization-first thinking that hurts users (and, one could argue, ultimately hurts the organizations that engage in it, too) is spending time and money on SEO tactics that attempt to game the system with endless amounts of low-quality content or cheap link-bait, rather than simply focusing efforts on creating the content your users want, delivering it in terms that fit their natural language, and using clean code to do it.

If your organization values these sorts of customer-unfriendly tactics above the customers themselves—talking more about lead generation than lead satisfaction—then it's going to be difficult to turn it into a future-thinking, adaptable business. After all, if you're too busy thinking about yourself, how can you make time to care about what others want?

What's a future-focused, customer-centric person like you to do? For starters, it's time to reframe your organization's internal conversation from one that's centered on the business and its desires to one that emphasizes users' goals and how the business can help them get there.

It also takes a concerted effort (and more than you alone) to break down silos, getting rid of the interdepartmental squabbles or inabilities to communicate that keep IT operating in complete ignorance of marketing; PR publishing content totally unaware of product reviews on social sites; and vice presidents demanding new documentation for initiatives that are seconds from becoming obsolete. After all, none of these communication challenges is actually about solving your customers' problems; instead, they're all about your organization's internal issues.

Ultimately, being customer-focused means being adaptable, and building business models that don't depend on a single piece of technology or a single department. It means happily giving users access to high-quality, easy-to-understand information—not controlling their experience with it. And it means expecting that users' expectations will change, and building a business that enables you to change with it.

After all, if you don't serve your customers, how can you expect them to stick around?

## Collaboration

Lack of collaboration takes many forms. Groups practice one-upmanship or seek to take all the credit for a joint effort. Interdepartmental meetings are painful, not productive. One discipline disparages the other, even when they can't actually function without them: "IT doesn't understand anything about our customers!" "You know how designers are, they just can't understand business."

Without a collaborative spirit, it's impossible to plan for and be successful at publishing content that works across devices and channels. After all, IT needs content folks to weigh in on CMS selection; IAs need technical teams to implement content models; and developers need folks to help them understand what the API needs to accomplish. The list could go on and on.

Thankfully, if you can get your organization to think about its customers, you can go a long way in solving the collaboration problem, too—because collaboration and customer centricity are really two sides of the same coin. That is, as you push your organization toward thinking about the customer in everything it does, those involved will naturally start working together more often, and with fewer failures to see eye to eye—because all parties will have the same focal point in mind: the customer.

Vision, customer focus, collaboration: Look carefully and you'll see that all three of these things really go hand in hand. At its core, the organization of the future must embrace the humans with whom it's trying to do business and give them the content they need to get things done. When an organization is ready to do that, then they'll do what it takes to make a change.

## Building a Team

If you're leading a group tasked with content-related work, you're in luck. Even if your organization is struggling to coalesce around a vision, collaborate, or consider its customers, you still have the opportunity to start making change happen—simply by the way you organize your team and approach your project.

Just look at what the U.S. government has done. While the president can make a mandate, it's not as if the White House can dictate every decision from the top down. The government is far too big and complex for that to work, and the administration has a few too many other issues on its plate.

Instead, a collaborative team from multiple agencies created the Digital Services Innovation Center, which is serving as a guide for the initiative, turning the big-picture vision into smaller, more manageable projects that can serve as examples and inspiration for further efforts—like the FCC's content API already has.

In so doing, the government isn't trying to tear down bureaucracy overnight; that would cause far too much disruption at once. Instead, it's building Web services like APIs that allow its content to *transcend* that bureaucracy—so the content can bridge the gaps between agencies, even if the agencies themselves are still siloed.

If you're trying to get your organization to start working more collaboratively, this might be your best approach. Rather than thinking of your team as needing to belong to one department, like "marketing" or "user experience," look for opportunities to make it more cross-functional and interdepartmental, pulling in people from different places. And even if your leadership isn't talking about customer-centric, open content, it probably can't avoid talking about things like mobile—and you can use that to your advantage in getting a team together. If you can make strides toward content that crosses departmental divides, it's only a matter of time before some of those siloes start breaking down, too.

This approach will also empower your team to bring the benefits of their content work to whatever part of the organization they're from—so small changes, perhaps even just to a single kind of content, can get noticed and built upon by other groups, creating the demand for further organizational change.

In this way, your goal probably isn't to dictate exactly how content models will get implemented and structured content stored across the whole organization. Rather, it's to be a role model and a resource for creating a foundation for adaptable, flexible content. It's to enable others to experiment—and get them excited about the possibilities.

If your team can do that, you've already succeeded. Because when people are excited, bigger changes are sure to come.

## Being on the Outside

This chapter has been especially focused on the inside of organizations, but that doesn't mean you're off the hook if you work in an agency or as a consultant. I've spent all the parts of my career that matter outside the bounds of a big organization. After many years of client meetings and trainings and recommendation documents, I know firsthand how difficult it can be to get an organization to adopt lasting change when you're presenting it from an external perspective. No matter what you know or how carefully you've researched, you're still a hired hand. And at some point, you'll go home.

If you're working on a client project—whether it's a website build, a CMS integration, a content audit, or a brand and messaging exercise—you can still start that client on a path toward change. But it might take a shakeup to the way you're used to selling your services.

Outside parties often come into an organization acting like suitors: You sweep the client off his feet, whisper in his ear, and tell him everything's going to be OK. In short, you make the sale because you make it sound easy for the client—like all he has to do is hire you and his messy content problems will go away. Poof.

Of course, they won't—not unless the organization also invests in the process of working with you to break down its chaotic business issues and rebuild an internal workflow that actually works for its content's future.

In short, your work to future-proof your clients' content will only be as successful as they choose to make it. And you can't expect them to make it so if you've sold them on a bright, shiny solution (like...ahem...a CMS), rather than on a process of change.

It's time for those of us who provide services to clients to stop with the flashy pitches and grand unveilings and start selling our work as what it is: outside perspective, practical expertise, and a commitment to helping them navigate the challenges of change.

## Dealing with Fear

If agencies and consultants get more honest about the often brain-crunching, time-consuming work required to make content...well...*work*, it'll scare off some potential clients. They won't be ready to break the status quo and invest in change, and the prospect of doing so will make them shut down.

Those organizations will hire an agency that will sell them on a solution, rather than one that admits how much work they'll have to put in. Accept this. Be thankful for this.

You don't want that client, because you can't actually help that client.

An organization that won't take a good, hard look at itself—yes, even that one with the really good brand name or the really cool product—isn't prepared for authentic, human, direct communication. It won't be ready to adapt itself to content that's unfixed and, in a sense, out of its control. It can't collaborate around a single vision for its future, because it's too busy worrying about the past.

Not every organization will make it, but don't despair. You now have the skills to help the worthy ones get there, and the tools to tell who is ready and who isn't.

## Putting People First

Whatever your organization's content challenges are, you can't solve them without putting people first—creating content that's for real humans, and that helps in real ways. Whenever that truth is forgotten or pushed aside because of departmental politics or short-term sales goals, your customers—and your organization—lose.

When you can work to align your organization around its customers, making them the "gravitation center" of your content, as Cameron Koczon called it in Chapter 11, you'll find it's a lot easier to make any future-facing content strategy get implemented better and engrained deeper.

As we'll talk about in our last chapter, staying human is also what will allow you to avoid some of the common pitfalls of modular, reusable, flexible content: becoming robotic, mechanical, and cold—pitfalls that could otherwise leave you just as stuck as before.

CHAPTER 13

# Towards a New (Information) Architecture

Designing for Change                                         204
Architecture from Within                                     205
The Problem with Mass Production                             207
Content in the Age of Mechanical Reproduction               208
Keeping the Aura Intact                                      209
Content for Humans                                           210
The Road Ahead                                               210

W e've spent the bulk of this book focused on establishing a methodology for organizing content: one based on meaning and purpose, on rules and relationships. We've explored practical approaches to making smart decisions about how to structure and store information. We've walked through examples of how others are creating more reusable, mobile-ready, flexible content.

And yet, this book isn't really about method; it's about mindset: about establishing a way of thinking that will serve your content—not to mention your users, your organization, and your sanity—well into the future. It's about building a framework for thinking about content, not answering every question you'll encounter about it.

After all, methods must adjust with time and technology, changing as new tools are built and new ideas developed. But a mindset that's flexible, more focused on retaining content's meaning and purpose than on defining its location, is what will allow you to adapt to whatever new methods come to pass.

This way of thinking—one where the structures we build derive from what our content means and how it means it, and where pages and documents give way to new forms and approaches—requires a fundamental shift in the way we think about and design for the Web, forcing us to take a fresh look at the very disciplines we've embraced as careers: the writing of documents, the architecting of information.

Changing how you work, and how you think, is no small task. So before I leave you to tackle your own organization's issues and break down your own blobs of content, let's take a moment to gain some inspiration from the past—and see how keeping a human focus in our work can help us avoid some of the pitfalls of modular, reusable content.

## Designing for Change

The Web moves quickly. Apps and mash-ups and services and sites launch daily. Bots continue to take over formerly human tasks. Devices hit shelves, make a splash, and then become obsolete within just a few months.

Things are shifting at a dizzying rate, and our customers and clients expect us to keep up. It's a tremendously exciting new world, and as we talked about in Chapter 12, "Content and Change," it's one where the only way not to let it run you ragged is to stop chasing after the newest new thing and start investing in solutions that are more scalable and adaptable.

In a sense, today's challenge isn't so different from what happened in the first part of the last century—a time when mechanization was rapidly changing the economic and social landscape, and people were struggling to make sense of the endless array of new technology around them.

Automobiles, airplanes, ocean liners: the technological advancements of the early 20th century set into motion a new way of thinking about building—moving focus toward engineering, repeatable processes, and modular parts, rather than on designing individual units as complete, immutable wholes.

In other words, people started thinking about how to design for a world that had changed.

## Architecture from Within

> The plan proceeds from the inside out; the exterior is the result of the interior.
>
> —Le Corbusier, 1923

Shaped by these advancements, and the changes they brought to everything from urban life to warfare, a new movement emerged in art and architecture: modernism. Perhaps the most prominent proponent of this new aesthetic in architecture was the French modernist Le Corbusier, known for his 1923 treatise *Towards an Architecture* (widely known, until its most recent scholarly English translation in 2007, as *Towards a New Architecture*). Reacting to the embellished, grandiose beaux-arts style that was en vogue at the start of the 20th century, Le Corbusier called for his peers to develop a new architecture—one focused on designing for purpose, rather than decoration (see Figure 13.1).

Calling the home a "machine for living in," Le Corbusier emphasized the importance of understanding purpose—of breaking homes down to their elements so that a new approach to designing spaces would emerge: spaces that could be mass produced, and whose structure would endure through those replications.

In this world, homes and communities would trade in decoration—flourishes that didn't contribute to practical living—for design that embraced the repeatable processes and standardized parts of the modern world.

As part of this new architecture, Le Corbusier envisioned mass-produced housing designed with various combinations of the same standardized fixtures and finishes, creating communities that could be built quickly and efficiently off the same modular designs.

Today, as the people responsible for designing the systems that will support content, our task in some ways isn't unlike that of Le Corbusier's mass-production housing. We must design our content's structure around its purpose, and make it modular and reusable across different applications.

FIGURE 13.1
Beaux-arts detail defines the New York Public Library, built in 1911.
Needless to say, Le Corbusier preferred the style of Villa Savoye, a modernist
home he built in Poissy, France, from 1928 to 1931 (image by Lawrence Baulch,
Creative Commons-BY).

# The Problem with Mass Production

Yet this aesthetic of modularity and mass production wasn't without its pitfalls—pitfalls we must avoid as we wrestle to make our reusable, replicable modules of content work for users.

In fact, Le Corbusier's harshest critics later accused his "new architecture" of leading to the rigid, uninviting structures of postwar communism in the East and public housing complexes in the cities of the West. In housing projects from East Berlin to East Harlem, millions of humans inhabited similarly towering, bleak buildings built—ostensibly at least—under the principles outlined by Le Corbusier: repeatability, efficiency, modularity (see Figure 13.2).

If the home is indeed a machine for living in, as Le Corbusier touted in *Towards an Architecture*, then these spaces seemed to define "living" in an incredibly limited way: They included all the necessary components, but none of the necessary life. Though repeatable everywhere and functionally complete, structures like these were devoid of spirit: disconnected from the cities in which they were located, isolating, and unfriendly for pedestrians— "in the city, but not of the city," as the popular saying goes.

FIGURE 13.2
East Harlem's Robert F. Wagner public housing project, built in 1958, presents a pretty bleak view of modular, repeatable structures (image by Madame Chaotica, Creative Commons-BY).

This is precisely what we need to avoid with our content. While we want the benefits of modular, reusable content, we're not running factories that stamp out the same chunks of content, day after day. Instead, as we talked about in Chapter 12, today's challenge is to be adaptable to a constantly changing landscape.

This means we need content that can be reused across different outputs, yet that feels not just *in* its medium, but *of* its medium, everywhere it goes. We need content that can feel in context with anywhere it's being presented, even if we don't know exactly where that might be yet.

Simultaneously, we need to keep our content's liveliness intact as it becomes modular and more automated—a challenge that has long plagued projects that seek to aggregate and collect like content, like the BBC's nature or recipe websites we learned about in Chapter 8, "Findable Content." Without a human editor shaping and guiding their production, what separates these hubs of information from a list of links, functionally just fine but practically quite boring?

## Content in the Age of Mechanical Reproduction

We're not the first to grapple with challenges like this. In his 1936 essay, "The Work of Art in the Age of Mechanical Reproduction," cultural critic Walter Benjamin argued that the effect of reproduction is often a loss of authenticity—that the "aura" that accompanied the original dissipates as it is copied.

Of course, neither Le Corbusier nor Benjamin could have foreseen today's world of digital content—a world where labels like "original" and "reproduction" are difficult to affix to information that's ultimately just an expression of ones and zeroes. Yet this idea that our work—call it art, call it content, call it product—has an aura, a sense of authenticity, is still quite valuable.

Like those acres of monolithic housing projects, carefully subdivided into endlessly replicable units, content that's devoid of liveliness and authenticity won't do us any good. As we move towards being more structured and modular, towards making things that can be repurposed and reconfigured over and over again, we must never lose sight of this need for feeling—lest we end up with content that's functionally adequate, yet unsatisfying and dead.

# Keeping the Aura Intact

As technological advancement continues rapidly for us, much like it did for the early modernists, we must learn to keep pace by designing new systems for content—without falling victim to this unaesthetic, cold industrialization. We must build an approach to our work that embraces standard, repeatable systems for content, without rendering that content devoid of the spirit that lends it meaning.

But in an age where reproduction is unavoidable, and even desirable, where and how does the aura—the heart and soul of the content—live? How do we mechanize the means by which our content is published without mechanizing the content itself?

The answer is in not just devising content structures that are universally recognizable, but that also retain their inherent brand, message, and art—the things that make the content itself any *good*.

This is the real crux of creating content that will endure, serving your organization and users into the future: it must shift and reshape to fit varied devices, contexts, and sites, while also retaining its essence—the substance that defines it and makes it what it is.

Getting closer to content and understanding how its elements lend it meaning and give it purpose, as we've learned to do throughout this book, is the only way to keep content from losing its power as its context shifts.

That's why it's so critical not to just model content in the technical sense, but to start with the creative sense, as we learned to do in Chapter 3, "Breaking Content Down." Because it's only once we understand what our content means for our users—and make structural decisions that support and enhance that meaning—that we'll make it strong enough to stay intact as it faces shifts in device, location, and layout.

This is also why we can't assume the same structuring, the same COPE model, or the same markup is going to work for everything and everyone. It's why single-sourcing all your content, all the time, is likely a pipe dream. And it's why so many structured content efforts have had a hard time gaining steam outside of niche technical groups.

Instead of looking at structure as a single solution—a one-size-fits-all approach to content—it's important to consider your content on a spectrum, from handcrafted to fully automated. Some content is truly just for one place, one moment in time. Some must be so human and in the moment that it can't be robotically yanked from a database and plopped onto a page.

That's OK.

The real work is in determining which things need that level of human care, and which things do not—and building systems that allow you to make it happen.

## Content for Humans

Whether it was a case of unforeseen consequences, bad implementation, or simply flawed ideas from the start, countless buildings were constructed with Le Corbusier's ideals in mind that stripped the humanness from living— treated a room's purpose as something cold, sterile, and purely task-oriented. And just as that failed to serve the needs of the people who inhabited these perfectly repeatable, infinitely modular homes, any approach that removes the human touch from our content will fail our users as well.

After all, our goal isn't to spread our content as far as possible, distributing its seeds onto each and every patch of land we can find. Content everywhere means, at its core, content that lives on, inhabiting many different lives across many different paths, not all of which we can control. It means content that flexes and fits our users, without breaking the things that make it what it is: its provenance, its message, its craft.

Content that has any hope of enduring—of making a lasting impression on a person's life, values, loyalties, or actions—must matter to the person consuming it. And that means it will never be enough to simply replicate information across every device, channel, platform, or touch point possible.

Instead, if you embrace this more micro approach to information architecture—considering the inherent shape of your content first, then designing human-centered systems that connect the dots and enable understanding— you'll be able to keep the heart of your content intact, wherever it goes.

## The Road Ahead

"Content" can be a dirty word. Vague and vast in its definition, it can come to include nearly anything and everything—so it's easy to dismiss or to stop bothering to parse its meaning.

But, as we've talked about time and again throughout this book, content isn't homogenous, each molecule the same. It's layered, rich, and intensely personal. It's expensive to create, time-consuming to keep up, and impossible to do without.

It's complex, and it deserves attention and analysis.

Yet we spend so much time thinking about content—full of powerful stories, important information, critical details—as just documents and pages, identical little units where each one is exactly like the others. We've failed to take its complexity into account when it comes to how we've published and displayed it. And as a more mobile, social, and user-centered Web has emerged, that failure has finally caught up with us.

It's time we right the ship.

Wherever the world goes with markup, whatever happens with the Semantic Web and APIs and even big hairy problems like media revenue models, the truth remains: You're going to need content that's ready for multiple destinations—multiple potential destinies.

In fact, if you even want to be part of your organization's conversations *about* those big hairy problems, you'd be best served by understanding your content and all the ways it might get used and reused.

To get there, you have to break down both your content and the organizational hurdles that are preventing your organization from change. You have to focus on getting modular and more flexible without losing sight of what your content means and how it matches your audiences' mental models.

Without this, it doesn't really matter whether you live and die by XML, demand a CMS that can handle markdown, or any number of other practical matters. You'll still be stuck dealing with content that doesn't stand the test of time, and your organization or client will still feel the pain of every new device and platform and expectation your users develop.

The Internet is going to change. The business world is going to change. And it's all going to happen very quickly, without a lot of time for big, bumbling slowpoke organizations to catch up. But your content doesn't have to be left behind. You can start working, right now, to help your organization or clients adapt more quickly, embrace new ideas more easily, and run more efficiently well into the future. You can make content that endures—content that withstands changes to how and where it's displayed, and still continues to serve its purpose.

If you do, you'll not only help your organization and its customers, but you'll also increase your job prospects—and likely your own professional satisfaction as well. If you don't, you'll end up stuck, too—unable to bring your skills and experience along as the future continues marching on.

The choice is yours, but the content isn't. It belongs to your users. It's time you give it to them, everywhere they want it.

# Index

## SYMBOLS

# (hash mark), for markdown, 104

## A

accessible information, 122
A-class data, 66
adaptive design, 138
*Adaptive Web Design* (Gustafson), 138
advertising, 176
  location of, 142
advertising-supported revenue
  model, 149
AJAX include pattern, 144
Amazon.com, 157–159
Android platform, 12
APIs (application programming interfaces), 110. *See also* content APIs
  advocating for, 117
  basics, 111
  of NPR, 23, 115–116
  public vs. private, 115–116
  read vs. write, 116
  reasons for adopting, 115
*APIs: A Strategy Guide* (Jacobson, Brail,
  and Woods), 111
AppendAround, 142
approvals, of content, 63
arizonaguide.com, 70
  template, 71
Arizona Office of Tourism, 65, 68
  content limitations, 69
Arizona State University, 146
  homepage, 4
art, content modeling as, 34–35
Atherton, Mike, 126–127, 131
atomizing content, 60
attributes
  in data model, 61
  identifying in content, 58
  keyword-rich, 123–124
  shared, for content hubs, 124
attribution, 182–183
attribution element, 45
authenticity, 208
author byline element, 69
authors, 45

experience, 22, 66
and workflows, 63–72

## B

Barker, Deane, 33, 56, 58–59
Benjamin, Walter, "The Work of
  Art in the Age of Mechanical
  Reproduction," 208
Berners-Lee, Tim, 102
Bing, 100
body content element, 45–46
*Boston Globe*, 142
Brail, Greg, *APIs: A Strategy Guide*, 111
Brand, Zach, 23, 44
British Broadcasting Corporation
  BBC Food, 124–125
  Wildlife Finder, 132, 133
bulleted lists, 45
business element, 70
business rules, framework for, 76
byline element, 45

## C

caption element, 46
captions, and photos, 8
cascading style sheets (CSS)
  for flexible content, 140
categories, 46
central content store, 155–156
change, 194–198, 211
  designing for, 204
  in organizations, 192
  vision and, 195–196
character types, for content types, 54
Cisco, 11
City element, 70
classes in HTML, 99
classification system, 55
Cloud Four, 104
Cognifide, 66
collaboration, 197–198
collaborative team, 198
Columbia University, 179, 180
compensation, for digital
  content, 184–185
complementary content element, 46

completeness, of CMS, 64
complexity
 flexibility vs., 56
 of content, 63
complexity, level of, 59
conditional statements, 89
conditions, 77. *See also* rules
connecting data, 10–11
consistency, 64
consultants, 199
content. *See also* reusable content
 artificial limitations, 146
 contextually discoverable, 131–133
 flexibility, 13
 in age of mechanical
   reproduction, 208
 intermixing, 141–142
 layering, 143–145
 making it work harder, 5–6
 making lightweight, 147
 meaning of, 210–211
 personalized, 162–163, 171
 quality of, 127, 187
 related and contextual, 79–82
 removing, 145–146
 reused, resized, and removed, 60
 separating structure from
   presentation, 19
 separation from presentation, 59
 size of, 85
 updates, 5
 value of, 192
content APIs, 111–114
 basics, 110–111
 government and education use of, 114
 major media organizations' use of,
   111–112
 retailers use of, 113
content architecture, 66
 fitting in container, 139
 from within, 205–206
content audits, 40–41
content chunks, 181
 breaking pages into, 11
content curation, 134
content elements, 31. *See also* elements
"content first" approach, 148

content hubs, 124–125
content management system
   (CMS), 21–26
 capabilities and trade-offs, 61–62
 evaluating existing, 63
 markup and, 98–99
 of NPR, 23
 template, 71
content models, 21, 31
 as art, 34–35
 as ecosystems, 73
 authors and workflows, 63–72
 basics, 52
 benefits, 30–31
 considerations and
   compromises, 56–60
 detail level in, 57
 documenting, 52–56
 examples, 36–39
 for NPR, 88
 gains and losses in, 56–57
 legacy systems, 64
 meaning before modeling, 31–33
content relevance, 129
content shifting
 basics, 175
 benefits, 178–179
 options for managing, 185–186
 problems from portability, 182–185
 taking advantage of, 179–182
content specialists, technical teams
   and, 67
content store, central, 155–156
content strategy, 5, 18–19, 39–42
 importance of developing, 160
*Content Strategy for Mobile*
   (McGrane), 160
*Content Strategy for the Web* (Halvorson), 5
content structure, 1, 179
 and findability, 122
 thinking about, 35
content types, 31, 35
 common, 42–43
 elements for connecting, 81
 priorities for search results, 129
 relationships, 53
 turning into elements, 43–44

contextual content, 79–82
COPE: Create Once, Publish Everywhere concept, 23–24
copy deck, 45, 69, 100
copyright, 184
customers
  focus on, 196–197
  request for information from, 196

## D

Darwin Information Type Architecture (DITA), 101
  prototyping, 20
data
  connecting, 10–11
  integration, APIs and, 111
  linked, 102, 103, 127
*Database Design for Mere Mortals*, 58
databases, legacy, 8
data storage and retrieval, 31
date stamp element, 45
dbPedia, 127
deconstructing, 30–31
descriptive information, metadata as, 55
design for change, 204–205
desktop version of websites
  for Starbucks, 86
  layouts, 85
  unnecessary content, 147
details, broad perspective vs., 192–193
diagram of content concept relationships, 53
digital content, compensation for, 184–185
"Digital Government: Building a 21st Century Platform to Better Serve the American People," 164
Digital Services Innovation Center, 198
disconnected stories, 80
DITA (Darwin Information Type Architecture), 101, 155
  prototyping, 20
documentation
  of content models, 31, 52–56
  technical, 155–156
domain-driven design, 126–127

Drupal content API module, 114
dynamically displayed content, 79

## E

East Harlem, Robert F. Wagner public housing project, 207
ecosystems, content models as, 73
editorial control, for NPR, 88
education, content API use by, 114
elements
  for connecting content types, 81
  of data model, 61
  distinctiveness of, 44
  granular considerations, 57
  meaning of, 89
  priority in layout, 89–90
  relationships, 90–91
  role of, and placement, 89
  turning content types into, 43–44
*The Elements of Content Strategy* (Kissane), 19
entities, in data model, 61
Epicurious.com, 37–39, 47, 90
experiencing art, 34
experimentation, 186
  in art, 34

## F

faceted search, 129–131
fafsa.ed.gov, 165
fair use, 184
FCC.gov, 114
fear, 200
Federal Communications Commission, 114
  personalized content project, 162–163
fields, content purpose in determining, 32
Filament Group, 142
filtering metadata support for options, 122
findability, 122
  content structure and, 122
  finding soul in, 134–135
  in site search, 128–129
  for search engines, 123–125
fixed webpages, 6, 8
Flexbox (Flexible Box Layout Module), 140

flexibility
  cascading style sheets for, 140
  complexity vs., 56
  in grid layouts, 83
  in content, 13
flu.gov, 166–168
focus, on customer, 196–197
framework for flexible content, 18
Free Application for Federal Student Aid
    site, 165
freeform tags, 77
Frost, Brad, 144
Future Friendly online store, 144

**G**

Gardner, Lyza, 104
Gibbon, Cleve, 66
Gimme Bar, 174
goals, in content strategy, 40
GoDaddy, 176, 177
Godin, Seth, 193
Google, 100
  on smartphone use for decisions, 145
  updates to cut down on webspam, 123
Google Trends, 124
government. *See* U.S. government
Gracey, R. Stephen, 32, 34
granularity
  in content types, 42
  of content model, 59
grid layouts, 140
  flexible, 83
Grigsby, Jason, 13
Gruber, John, 104
*Guardian*, 168–170
Gustafson, Aaron, *Adaptive Web
    Design*, 138

**H**

Halvorson, Kristina, *Content Strategy for
    the Web*, 5
hash mark (#), for markdown, 104
Hay, Stephen, 150
headline element, 45, 69
hierarchical sitemaps, 126
hierarchical system, 79

history of content, 63
HTML5 microdata extension, 100
HTML markup, 99–100
hubs of content, 124–125

**I**

ideas, letting go of outdated, 187
identifiers, in data model, 62
image element, 46, 69
  for Epicurious element, 91
information
  accessible, 122
  elements representing unit of, 44
information architecture, 20–21
  of NPR, 23
Instapaper, 174, 179, 181
interdigitation, 141–142
intermixing content, 141–142
internal search engine, 128
iPhone apps, 12
  barcode scanner, 157–158
iPhone, Starbucks page display on, 85

**J**

Jacobson, Daniel, *APIs: A Strategy Guide*, 111
JavaScript, 142
JavaScript Object Notation (JSON), 101

**K**

key messages, in content strategy, 40
keyword-rich attributes, 123–124
keywords, research on, 124
keyword-stuffing, 123
Kindle Single, 186
Kissane, Erin, *The Elements of Content
    Strategy*, 19
KISS Metrics study, 147
Koczon, Cameron, 175, 200
Kottke, Jason, 134

**L**

labeling, 88
  content purpose in determining, 32
layering content, 143–145
lazy loading, 147

Le Corbusier
  critics of new architecture, 207
  *Towards an Architecture*, 205
legacy content models, 64
legacy databases, 8
length requirements, for content
  types, 54
*Letting Go of the Words: Writing Web
  Content that Works* (Redish), 5
lightweight content, 147
*Linchpin: Are You Indispensable?*
  (Godin), 193
linked data, 102, 103, 127
Linnaean taxonomy of animal
  kingdom, 55, 132
lists, bulleted or numbered, 45
loanconsolidation.ed.gov, 166

## M

*Managing Enterprise Content* (Rockley), 154
manual content, 79
manual tagging, 8
many-to-many relationships, 53
Marcotte, Ethan, 13, 82, 142
  *Responsive Web Design*, 138
markdown, 104–105
markup
  approaches, 106
  content management system and,
    98–99
  HTML, 99–100
  importance of, 96
  meanings and, 96–98
  presentational, 97, 98
  semantic, 97–98, 99–104
  structural, 100–102
Marquis, Mat, 147
mash-ups
  APIs and, 111
mass production, problem with,
  207–208
McGrane, Karen, 21, 30, 76, 158,
  160–161
  *Content Strategy for Mobile*, 160
meaning, 141
  of elements, 89

for Epicurious element, 91
markup and, 96–98
before modeling, 31–33
mechanical reproduction, content in
  age of, 208
metadata, 55, 76
  freeform, 77
  markup for, 96
  support for sort and filter options, 122
microdata, HTML5 extension, 100
microformats, 99
'micro' information architectures, 21
mindset, 204
mobile content
  appearance, 7
  impact of shift to, 67
mobile devices
  focus on, 160
  getting started on content for, 161
  individual variations in use, 145–146
  native applications for, 146
  StatCounter on internet usage, 11–12
*Mobile First* (Wroblewski), 12
Morville, Peter, 20
multichannel content, impact of
  shift to, 67
MusicBrainz, 127
my.fcc.gov, 162–163

## N

National Public Radio (NPR), 22–24, 44
  APIs use by, 115–116, 117
  content API use by, 111–112
  content models and rules, 88
National Student Loan Data System, 165
native applications, for mobile device
  users, 146
Netflix
  API use by, 113
New York Public Library, 206
*New York Times*, 103
  content API use by, 111–112
Notre Dame, 143–144
  location-aware features on website, 150
nslds.ed.gov, 165
numbered lists, 45

## O

one-to-many relationships, 53
one-to-one relationships, 53
orbital content, 175
organizations, change in, 192, 193
outside parties, interaction with
    organization, 199
OWL (Web ontology language), 101

## P

pages
    breaking into chunks, 11
    limitations, 8, 12
Parks, Todd, 164
PDFs, for government documents, 166
personalized collections of content, 171
personalized content, 162–163
personalized content centers, user
    creation, 162
perspective, broad vs. details, 192–193
Pew Research Institute, 11
photos, and captions, 8
Pinterest, 174, 182–183
Pocket, 174
Popova, Maria, 134
portable content, 175. *See also* content
    shifting
    problems from, 182–185
presentational markup, 97, 98
presentation of content
    separating from content, 59
    separating from structure, 19
press releases, 128–129
PriceCheck, 157–158
priorities, 65
    for Epicurious element, 91
    of content types for search results, 129
    of element in layout, 89–90
private APIs
    Amazon use of, 157
    public vs., 115–116
process, adapting, 33
product database, API for using, 113
products
    content across, 156–159
    delivering, 89

public APIs, private vs., 115–116
publishers, challenges, 160
pull quotes, 8, 46

## Q

quality content, 6

## R

rankings, on Web search engines, 123
ratings element, for Epicurious element, 91
RDF (Resource Description Framework),
    101
Readability, 174, 184–185
read APIs, write vs., 116
reading, improving the experience, 186
Read it Later, 174
recipes, content model for, 36
Redish, Ginny, *Letting Go of the Words:
    Writing Web Content that Works*, 5
related content, 79–82
relational databases, custom-built, 58
relationships
    in data model, 61
    for Epicurious elements, 91
    of content types, 53
    of elements, 90–91
    rules as basis, 81
relevance of content, 129
repository, 156
reproduction rights, 184
research, on keywords, 124
Resnick, Ethan, 76
resources
    in content strategy, 40
responsive and adaptive design, 138–151
responsive design, 138
    adding content, 150
    simplicity in, 148
*Responsive Web Design* (Marcotte), 138
retailers, content APIs use by, 113
reusable content, 18, 154–171
    central content store, 155–156
    chasing perfection in, 170
    making meaningful, 171
    across products, 156–159
    revisiting, 154–155
    from U.S. government, 163–168

revenue model,
    advertising-supported, 149
Robert F. Wagner public housing project
    (East Harlem), 207
Rockley, Ann, *Managing Enterprise
    Content*, 154
role-based authoring, 66
Rosenfeld, Louis, 20
    *Search Analytics for Your Site: Conversa-
    tions with Your Customers*, 128
RSS (real simple syndication), 116
rules, 77–78
    for NPR, 88
    framework for making, 88–91
    implementing, 92
    importance of, 79–82
    intrinsic nature of, 78
    for responsive design, 82–87
    to create systems, 77
Rusbridger, Alan, 168

## S

Safari's Reader, 174
Schema.org, 100
screen size, and priority shift, 83
Seabourne Consulting, 114
search
    and content modeling, 57
    faceted, 129–131
    visibility in, 125
*Search Analytics for Your Site:
    Conversations with Your Customers*
    (Rosenfeld), 128
search engine optimization (SEO),
    124, 127
    tactics gaming system, 196
search engines
    common language for, 100
    findability for, 123–125
semantic markup, 97–98, 99–104, 140
Semantic Web, 102–104, 127
SFGate.com, 176, 177
shared attribute, for content hubs, 124
sharing content, 178
shopping, APIs for, 113
sidebar element, 46

sidebars, 79, 131
    Starbuck's rule for, 87
siloed information, 5, 194
simplicity, 148–150
single-sourcing, 209
site architecture, 79
site search, findability, 128–129
smartphones, 12
    ownership statistics, 145
    use for decisions, 145
smartphone-sized displays, 85
social platforms, 12
sorting
    and content modeling, 57
    metadata support for options, 122
source-order independence, 140
spreadsheets, for content types, 54
Starbucks, 83–87
    desktop-sized layout, 86
    rule for sidebar, 87
StatCounter, on mobile Internet usage,
    11–12
static content, 79
statistics, on smartphone
    ownership, 145
structural markup, 100–102
structure of content, 30, 179
    separating from presentation, 19
    substance and, 47
subhead element, 45
substance, structure and, 47
summary element, 45
sustainability, 195
Svpply, 174, 178
synopsis element, 45
systems, rules to create, 77

## T

tablet-sized layouts, 85
tag cloud, 77
tags, 46
    freeform, 77
    manual, 8
taxonomies, 55
    of content types, 100
team building, 198–199

teaser copy, for Epicurious element, 91
teaser element, 45
technical communications, 19–20
technical documentation, 155–156
technical teams, content specialists
    and, 67
technological innovation, 209
    creating new framework, 14
templates
    arizonaguide.com, 71
    for Starbucks, 85
    users completion of, 64
theme element, 70
thinking, 204
time-shifted content, 175
title element, 45
tone, in content strategy, 40
*Towards an Architecture*
    (Le Corbusier), 205
training programs, for CMS users, 64
transcript element, 46

## U

U.S. government, 193–194
    change to customer service
        culture, 194
    content API use by, 114
    digital content, 164
    reusable content from, 163–168
University of Notre Dame, 143–144
    location-aware features on
        website, 150
user experience, 22
user interface copy, 43
users
    focus on, 196–197
    locations for acquiring
        content, 176–178
    personalized collections of content, 171
    perspective in evaluating content, 44

## V

value of content, 192
video element, 46
visibility in search, 125
vision, and change, 195–196
voice, in content strategy, 40

## W

Walton, Trent, 139, 141
Web ontology language (OWL), 101
webpage, fixed, 6
websites
    search findability, 128–129
    thinking beyond, 11–12
webspam, 123
Web standards, 12–13
Windowshop, 157
Woods, Dan, *APIs: A Strategy Guide*, 111
Wordtracker, 124
workflows, authors and, 63–72
write APIs, read vs., 116
Wroblewski, Luke, 13, 146, 147
    *Mobile First*, 12
WYSIWYG
    (what-you-see-is-what-you-get), 6

## X

XML (Extensible Markup Language), 20, 101

## Y

Yahoo!, 100

## Z

Zappos, 113, 130
Zeldman.com, 148
Zeldman, Jeffrey, 13, 148, 149
ZIP codes, 82

# ACKNOWLEDGMENTS

I'm indebted to everyone who listened to my excessive freak-outs, silenced my inner critic, and encouraged me enough to keep chipping away at this book. And trust me, that's a *lot* of people.

I'd especially like to thank Kristina Halvorson, who encouraged me to do this and introduced me to Lou Rosenfeld when I least expected it. Without that hearty shove, who knows what I'd be doing right now.

Lou Rosenfeld is the sort of guy you want in your corner: unflappable, above-board, and smart as hell. I'm lucky he believed I could pull this off, despite having precious little evidence to support my case. I'm also incredibly thankful for the whole Rosenfeld Media family: Marta Justak, my editor; Karen Corbett, who wrangles operations; the editorial board, who saw promise in my proposal; and the entire production team, who pulled all this together.

Eva-Lotta Lamm has a hyphenated German name, which means I liked her even before she created the incredible illustrations used in this book.

I would never have finished the manuscript without the support of the nitpicky and crazy smart Jonathan Kahn, as well as my other reviewers Jason Grigsby, Elisabeth Hubert, Erin Kissane, and Sarah Krznarich. Their detailed, thoughtful feedback pushed me in all the right ways, as did the support of early readers Margot Bloomstein, Dan Klyn, Rachel Lovinger, Ethan Marcotte, and Ginny Redish.

Karen McGrane, Ann Rockley, Deane Barker, Mike Atherton, Cleve Gibbon, and R. Stephen Gracey contributed material that brought new perspective to the book—and influenced my writing and thinking as well.

Friends like Anna Hrach, Eric Covill, Daniel Eizans, Nicole Jones, Matt Grocki, Deb Gelman, Corey Vilhauer, Carolyn Wood, Tim Kadlec, Boon Sheridan, and Chris Avore gave me endless encouragement, advice, and criticism throughout the process.

And then there was a whole cast and crew of delightful folks who shared their expertise and experiences with me: Zach Brand and Patrick Cooper at NPR, Mike Reich at Seaborne Consulting and his client at the FCC, Gray Brooks. Mark Porter talked with me about the *Guardian*; Erik Runyon gave me insight into Notre Dame's website; Dave Olsen and his team shared their experiences at West Virginia University.

The list goes on: Aaron Gustafson, Cameron Koczon, Dorian Taylor, Jeff Eaton, Jeffrey MacIntyre, John Eckman, Josh Clark, Lyza Gardner, MaryLee Grant, Mat Marquis, Max Fenton, Stephen Hay, Michael Spinnella, and Scott Abel all took the time to talk with me and make me much, much smarter than I was before.

But I can't thank anyone more than William Bolton, my partner and best friend for the past decade, who managed to defend his doctoral dissertation and move us across the country while I was writing this book. His patience and love have made this possible.

Thank you all.

—Sara Wachter-Boettcher
Lancaster, Pennsylvania, September 2012

# ABOUT THE AUTHOR

 **Sara Wachter-Boettcher** is an independent content strategist, writer, editor, and consultant. She got this way after stints as a journalist, copywriter, and Web writer, during which she became increasingly dissatisfied with the chaos typically found in Web content projects. In 2008, she launched a content strategy practice at her past agency, and started working closely with IA and UX teams to build a better way forward.

Today, Sara focuses on designing systems for flexible, adaptable content, with a heavy interest in making content mobile-ready and future-friendly. When she's not consulting with clients or partnering with agencies, she's serving as editor in chief of *A List Apart*, contributing to publications like *Contents* magazine, and speaking about content strategy, user experience, and related topics at conferences worldwide. You can read more at sarawb.com.

CPSIA information can be obtained
at www.ICGtesting.com
Printed in the USA
JSHW040751220123
36566JS00004B/5